Instant Pot

Cookbook for Beginners 2024

Super Easy Speedy & Tasty Instant Pot Recipes to Save Busy Life and Eating Well, Step By Step Instruction for Smart Cooking

Evelyn H. Perez

Copyright Statement and Disclaimer

Dear Reader,

Thank you for choosing to explore the culinary journey presented within the pages of this recipe book. We want to share our passion for food with you while also ensuring clarity about the rights, responsibilities, and expectations that come with using this book.

Copyright Notice

This recipe book is a labor of love, and its contents are protected by copyright law. ©2024 Evelyn H. Perez. All Rights Reserved. This means that all the recipes, instructions, photographs, and other content within this book are the intellectual property of the author and/or publisher and are legally protected. We kindly request your respect for these rights.

Legal notice. This book is protected by copyright. It is intended for personal use only. You may not modify, distribute, sell, use, quote or paraphrase any part or content of this book without the consent of the author or publisher.

By using this recipe book, you agree to abide by the terms outlined in this copyright statement and disclaimer.

Warmest wishes,

Evelyn H. Perez

CONTENTS

INTRODUCTION 9
How does Instant Pot work? 10
Instant pot parts 10
Instant pot dos and don'ts 11
How do I clean my Instant Pot? 12

Breakfast 14
Lemony Pancake Bites With Blueberry Syrup 14
Bacon Onion Cheddar Frittata 14
Western Omelet Casserole 14
Banana & Vanilla Pancakes 15
Tofu Hash Brown Breakfast 15
Cinnamon Roll Doughnut Holes 15
Sausage And Sweet Potato Hash 15
Egg Muffins To Go 16
Pumpkin Steel Cut Oats With Cinnamon 16
Banana Nut Bread Oatmeal 16
Savory Roast Beef Sandwiches 16
Tex-mex Breakfast 17
Hard-"boiled" Eggs 17
Crustless Crab Quiche 17
Chicken Sandwiches With Barbecue Sauce 18
Blueberry-oat Muffins 18
Honey Butternut Squash Cake Oatmeal 18
Vanilla Chai Latte Oatmeal 19
Pumpkin Spice Latte French Toast Casserole 19
Strawberry Jam 19
Sweet Potato Morning Hash 19
Tomato Mozzarella Basil Egg Bites 20
Ham And Swiss Muffin Frittatas 20
California Frittata Bake 20
Speedy Soft-boiled Eggs 21
Greek Yogurt With Honey & Walnuts 21
Bacon Cheddar Scrambled Egg Muffins 21
Breakfast Frittata 21
Trail Mix Oatmeal 22
Crustless Power Quiche 22
Peachy Cream Oats 22

Appetizers, Soups & Sides 23
Delicious Pork & Garbanzo Bean Chili 23
Cauliflower & Potato Soup With Parsley 23
Crushed Potatoes With Aioli 23
Chorizo Soup With Roasted Tomatoes 23

Tangy Egg Snacks	24
Savory Butternut Squash Soup	24
Frittata With Vegetables & Cheese	24
Creamy Creamed Corn	25
Garlicky Mashed Root Vegetables	25
Twice-baked Potatoes	25
Pork Ribs With Onions	26
Chili Corn On The Cob	26
Happy Dip	26
Sumac Red Potatoes	26
Vegetarian Soup With White Beans	26
Spicy Chicken Chili	27
Italian-style Brussels Sprouts	27
Goat Cheese & Beef Steak Salad	27
Homemade Vichyssoise Soup With Chives	27
Pea & Beef Stew	28
Asian-style Chicken Soup	28
Picante Chicken Wings	28
Nutty Potatoes	28
Steamed Broccoli	29
Sparerib Nachos	29
Four Cheeses Party Pizza	29
Mediterranean Soup With Tortellini	29
Chicken & Noodle Soup	30
Potato & Broccoli Soup With Rosemary	30
Beanless Chili	30
Sausage & Egg Casserole	31

Beans, Rice, & Grains 32

Risotto With Spring Vegetables & Shrimp	32
One-pot Mexican Rice	32
Hawaiian Rice	32
Primavera Egg Noodles	32
Cranberry Millet Pilaf	33
Beef Pasta Alla Parmigiana	33
Quinoa Bowls With Broccoli & Pesto	33
Cheeseburger Macaroni	33
Spicy Linguine With Cherry Tomato & Basil	34
Chicken & Broccoli Rice	34
Boston Baked Beans	34
Provençal Rice	35
Garlic Mushroom Polenta	35
Rice & Chicken Soup	35
Rice & Red Bean Pot	35
Parmesan Risotto	36
Basic Basmati White Rice	36
Mustard Macaroni & Cheese	36
Mom's Black-eyed Peas With Garlic & Kale	36

Broccoli & Pancetta Carbonara 37
Asparagus Pasta With Pesto Sauce 37
Ziti Green Minestrone 37
Kiwi Steel Cut Oatmeal 37
Chickpea & Jalapeño Chicken 38
Creamed Lentils 38
Bulgur Pilaf With Roasted Bell Peppers 38
Weeknight Baked Beans 39
South American Pot 39
Cajun Red Beans 39
Honey Coconut Rice 39
Lime Brown Rice 40

Vegan & Vegetarian 41
Vegan Sloppy Joe's 41
Cauliflower Rice With Peas & Chili 41
Acorn Squash With Sweet Glaze 41
Black Bean Slider Patties 41
Grandma's Asparagus With Feta & Lemon 42
Traditional Italian Pesto 42
Spicy Split Pea Stew 42
Easy Tahini Sweet Potato Mash 42
Spicy Shiitake Mushrooms With Potatoes 43
Hot Tofu Meatballs 43
Stuffed Bell Peppers 43
Cannellini Beans With Garlic & Leeks 43
English Vegetable Potage 44
Tex-mex Quinoa 44
Cauliflower & Potato Curry With Cilantro 44
Sweet Potato Chili 45
Savory Spinach With Mashed Potatoes 45
Parsley Lentil Soup With Vegetables 45
Roman Stewed Beans With Tomatoes 45
Quinoa With Brussels Sprouts & Broccoli 46
Delicious Mushroom Goulash 46
Quick Cassoulet 46
Cheddar Cheese Sauce With Broccoli 46
Celery & Red Bean Stew 47
Coconut Milk Yogurt With Honey 47
Seasoned Black Beans 47
Parmesan Topped Vegetable Mash 48
Cauliflower Charcuterie 48
Mushroom & Ricotta Cheese Manicotti 48
Homemade Gazpacho Soup 48
Carrot & Chickpea Boil With Tomatoes 49

Fish & Seafood 50

Paprika Salmon With Dill Sauce 50
Mediterranean Cod With Capers 50
Easy Seafood Paella 50
Herby Crab Legs With Lemon 50
Chinese Shrimp With Green Beans 51
Galician-style Octopus 51
Basil Clams With Garlic & White Wine 51
Buttery Cod With Scallions 51
Steamed Halibut Packets 52
Party Shrimp With & Rice Veggies 52
Cilantro Cod On Millet With Peppers 52
Tilapia Fillets With Hazelnut Crust 52
Herbed Poached Salmon 53
Littleneck Clams In Garlic Wine Broth 53
Steamed Shrimp And Asparagus 53
Stuffed Tench With Herbs & Lemon 53
Low-country Boil 54
Herby Trout With Farro & Green Beans 54
Savory Cod Fillets In Maple-lemon Sauce 54
Quick Shrimp Gumbo With Sausage 55
Jalapeño Shrimp With Herbs & Lemon 55
Cheesy Shrimp Scampi 55
Seafood Pilaf 55
Creole Seafood Gumbo 56
Mussels With Lemon & White Wine 56
Red Onion Trout Fillets With Olives 56
Orange Roughy With Zucchini 56
Creamed Crab 57
Trout In Herb Sauce 57
Chili Squid 57
Red Wine Squid 58

Poultry 59

Chicken Wings In Yogurt-garlic Sauce 59
Chicken Taco Salad Bowls 59
Hungarian-style Turkey Stew 59
Honey-lemon Chicken With Vegetables 59
Turkey Cakes With Ginger Gravy 60
Turkey Sausage With Brussels Sprouts 60
Dijon Mustard Chicken Breast 60
Pumpkin & Wild Rice Cajun Chicken 61
Fennel Chicken With Tomato Sauce 61
Rosemary Chicken With Asparagus Sauce 61
Chicken Salad 62
Savory Orange Chicken 62
Cumin Chicken With Capers 62
Crispy Bacon & Bean Chicken 62
Chicken Fricassee 63

Tasty Indian Chicken Curry 63
Spicy Ground Turkey Chili With Vegetables 63
Chicken & Quinoa Soup 64
Indian-style Chicken 64
Herby Chicken With Peach Gravy 64
Chicken Drumsticks In Sriracha Sauce 65
Easy Pesto Chicken And Red Potatoes 65
Sweet & Spicy Bbq Chicken 65
Best Italian Chicken Balls 65
Chicken Alla Diavola 66
Chicken With Honey-lime Sauce 66
Chicken & Vegetable Stew 66
Buttermilk Cornish Game Hens 67
Creamy Mascarpone Chicken 67
Insalata Caprese Chicken Bowls 67
Tasty Chicken Breasts With Bbq Sauce 68

Pork, Beef & Lamb 69

Spiced Pork With Orange & Cinnamon 69
Green Pea & Beef Ragout 69
Shroomy Meatballs 69
Carnitas Lettuce Wraps 70
Carrot Casserole With Beef & Potato 70
Beef Arancini With Potatoes 70
Seasoned Boneless Pork Loin 70
Italian Meatballs With Pomodoro Sauce 71
Korean Short Ribs 71
Vegetable Casserole With Smoked Bacon 71
T-bone Steaks With Basil & Mustard 72
Spicy Lamb & Bean Chili 72
Vegetable & Lamb Casserole 72
Mongolian Beef Bbq 72
Vietnamese-style Rice Noodle Soup 73
Sambal Beef Noodles 73
Chorizo With Macaroni & Cheddar Cheese 73
Pulled Bbq Beef 74
Quick French-style Lamb With Sesame 74
Tandoori Pork Butt 74
Cumin Pork Chops With Peach Sauce 75
Garlic & Thyme Pork 75
Cajun Pork Carnitas 75
Apricot Jam-glazed Ham 76
Southern Pot Roast With Pepperoncini 76
Red Wine Beef & Vegetable Hotpot 76
Classic Pork Goulash 76
Beef Shawarma Bowls 77
Eggplant & Beef Stew With Parmesan 77
Moroccan Beef & Cherry Stew 77

Fruity Pork Steaks 78

Desserts & Drinks 79
After-dinner Boozy Hot Cocoa 79
Rice Pudding 79
Peanut Butter Custards 79
Chocolate Quinoa Bowl 79
Walnut & Pumpkin Tart 80
Pie Cups With Fruit Filling 80
Banana Bread Pudding 80
Homemade Lemon Cheesecake 81
Chocolate Glazed Cake 81
Catalan-style Crème Brûlée 81
Yogurt Cheesecake With Cranberries 82
Molten Chocolate Cake 82
Steamed Bread Pudding 82
Best Tiramisu Cheesecake 83
Strawberry Upside-down Cake 83
Peanut Butter Chocolate Cheesecake 83
Simple Apple Cinnamon Dessert 84
Homemade Walnut Layer Cake 84
Grandma's Fruit Compote 84
Easy Lemon Cake 85
Simple Lemon Cheesecake 85
Quick Coconut Treat With Pears 85
Root Beer Float Cupcakes 85
Simple Apple Cider With Orange Juice 86
Pineapple Upside-down Cake 86
Stuffed Apples 86
Pumpkin Cheesecake 87
Lemon-apricot Compote 87
Plum & Almond Dessert 87
Creme Caramel With Whipped Cream 87
Homemade Spanish-style Horchata 88

APPENDIX A: Measurement 89

APPENDIX B: Recipes Index 91

INTRODUCTION

Hello, I'm Evelyn H. Perez, and I'm thrilled to introduce you to my Instant Pot Cookbook. With a background in culinary arts and a passion for creating delicious, wholesome meals, I've spent years perfecting recipes that not only taste amazing but are also easy to prepare. My career in the culinary world has been a journey of exploration and experimentation, and I'm excited to share the fruits of that journey with you in this cookbook.

The purpose behind my cookbook is simple: to empower home cooks like you to make the most of your Instant Pot. I understand that busy lifestyles often leave little time for elaborate cooking, which is why I've crafted recipes that are not only flavorful but also quick and convenient. In this cookbook, you'll find step-by-step instructions for each recipe, making it easy for even beginners to follow along. I've included shopping lists to simplify your grocery trips, cooking times to help you plan your meals, and practical tips that I've picked up along the way to ensure your Instant Pot cooking experience is a breeze. It's my hope that this cookbook becomes your trusted companion in the kitchen, inspiring you to create wholesome, mouthwatering dishes with ease.

My hope is that this Instant Pot Cookbook becomes your trusted companion in the kitchen, making cooking a fun and rewarding experience. Whether you're a seasoned cook looking to simplify your meals or a novice eager to explore the world of culinary delights, I invite you to embark on this culinary journey with me. Here's to creating delicious, homemade meals that nourish both body and soul. Happy cooking!

How does Instant Pot work?

Instant Pot is a pressure cooker -- and then some. It also sautés, slow cooks, makes rice and steams veggies and poultry. It's an all-in-one device, so you can, for instance, brown a chicken and cook it all in the same pot. In most cases, Instant Pot meals are ready to serve in less than an hour.

Its quick cook times are thanks to its pressure-cooking function, which locks steam created by liquid (even liquid released from meat and veggies), building pressure and pushing steam back into the food.

But don't confuse it with a stovetop pressure cooker. Unlike your grandparents' pressure cooker, this Instant Pot eliminates safety concerns with a lid that locks, and stays locked, until the pressure is released.

Instant pot parts

Cooker Base pot with a heating element on the inside and a control panel on the front. This part doesn't go in the dishwasher, just so we're clear!

Inner Pot is where the food goes in. It's made from stainless steel and comes out; it can be cleaned by hand or in a dishwasher.

The lid – which has a sealing ring on the inside that keeps all the pressure and steam in the pot, as well as the following key features on top that you will use on regular basis.

Instant pot dos and don'ts

Instant Pot Don'Ts

DON'T BE AFRAID

You have absolutely no reason to be afraid of your Instant Pot. You may have heard horror stories of the original pressure cookers, but your Instant Pot has several safety features making it completely safe to use.

DON'T PUT ANYTHING ON THE PRESSURE RELEASE VALVE

This is a huge no-no. Even draping something over it when you release it is just not safe. This is because the release valve was designed to release the pressure upwards, and putting anything over it prevents that from happening. Not only is it unsafe, but it can damage your pressure cooker.

When opening the steam release valve, you may use an oven mit, but remove it as soon as you turn the valve to release the pressure.

DON'T PUT IT UNDER CABINETS

As difficult as this may be, you don't want your Instant Pot to be underneath your cabinets. The steam that is released from your pressure cooker is super hot. This steam can damage your cabinets when it is released.

DON'T PUT THE THING ON YOUR STOVE

Most severe malfunctions happen because of people putting their Instant Pot on the stove and accidently turning the burners on. Not only can this cause your Instant Pot to explode while its on, but it will damage your machine.

DON'T OVERFILL THE POT

The rule of pressure cooking is to not fill the pot more than halfway. If you have too much in your Instant Pot, the valves can clog and your seals may leak. Additionally, things like beans and rice need room to expand.

Instant Pot Do's

DO CHECK YOUR SEALING RING

Your Instant Pot lid will come with a sealing ring already installed in the lid. It will also come with an extra one. Make sure the sealing ring is in the right place and pushed all the way down and around the edge of the lid.

DO CLEAN YOUR INSTANT POT PROPERLY

Not cleaning your pressure cooker can decrease the life of your machine. Additionally, it can cause it not to work right or malfunction. Make sure you clean the inner pot, lid, and sealing ring, the outside of the pot, and get food particles out of the cracks and crevices.

DO CHECK THE POWER CORD

The power cord is detachable for cleaning purposes. Make sure the cord is connected to the Instant Pot securely before trying to use your pressure cooker. If it isn't, it could cause a short and destroy your machine.

DO BE CAREFUL WITH MILK PRODUCTS

Dairy products tend to curdle in the Instant Pot unless the recipe is followed precisely. Therefore, it is important to be careful when cooking anything that has dairy in it. Most of the time, you will want to find a recipe that has you put the dairy products in AFTER your pressure cook your food. However, there are Instant Pot Cheesecake and other recipes that require you to pressurize the dairy products. Be sure to follow the recipes exactly.

How do I clean my Instant Pot?

How Often to Clean an Instant Pot

Your Instant Pot should be cleaned after every use. Since most inner cooking chambers are made of stainless steel, the vessel can be hand-washed with hot water and dishwashing liquid, or placed in the dishwasher. The silicone seal can also be placed on the top rack of the dishwasher after each use. If the appliance is used regularly, it should be deep cleaned at least once a month.

1. Unplug the Instant Pot

When cleaning any small electrical appliance, always unplug the unit from the electrical outlet first, before cleaning.

2. Wash the Interior Cooking Vessel

After use, allow the stainless steel inner chamber to cool to room temperature. Use a plastic or rubber spatula to remove any excess food. Next, either hand wash the chamber with hot water and dishwashing liquid or place it in an automatic dishwasher. Also, wash the steaming rack if you used it during food preparation.

3. Clean the Inside Seal and Lid

Remove the silicone seal from the unit's lid and wipe down the interior of the lid with a damp sponge. The seal can be hand-washed with hot water and dish soap, or placed on the upper rack of the dishwasher. Set the cycle on the highest heat, or use the sanitizing cycle on your dishwasher.

4. Wipe Down the Cooker Base

Use a slightly damp sponge or dishcloth to wipe down the inside and outside of the cooker base, removing food splatters and spills. Use a little vinegar placed on a soft cloth for a streak-free shine on the outside.

5. Dry and Reassemble

Dry all of the components with a microfiber towel, or allow the unit to air-dry. Reassemble the lid with its silicone seal. The Instant Pot should be completely dry before storing it.

Breakfast

Lemony Pancake Bites With Blueberry Syrup

Servings: 4
Cooking Time: 24 Minutes
Ingredients:
- 1 packet Hungry Jack buttermilk pancake mix
- ⅔ cup whole milk
- Juice and zest of ½ medium lemon
- ⅛ teaspoon salt
- 1 cup water
- ½ cup blueberry syrup

Directions:
1. Grease a seven-hole silicone egg mold.
2. In a medium bowl, combine pancake mix, milk, lemon juice and zest, and salt. Fill egg mold with half of batter.
3. Add water to the Instant Pot and insert steam rack. Place filled egg mold on steam rack. Lock lid.
4. Press the Manual or Pressure Cook button and adjust time to 12 minutes. When timer beeps, quick-release pressure until float valve drops. Unlock lid.
5. Allow pancake bites to cool, about 3 minutes until cool enough to handle. Pop out of mold. Repeat with remaining batter.
6. Serve warm with syrup for dipping.

Bacon Onion Cheddar Frittata

Servings: 4
Cooking Time: 12 Minutes
Ingredients:
- 6 large eggs
- 2 teaspoons Italian seasoning
- ½ cup shredded Cheddar cheese
- ½ teaspoon salt
- ¼ teaspoon ground black pepper
- 1 tablespoon olive oil
- 4 slices bacon, diced
- 1 small yellow onion, peeled and diced
- 1 cup water

Directions:
1. In a medium bowl, whisk together eggs, Italian seasoning, cheese, salt, and pepper. Set aside.
2. Press the Sauté button on the Instant Pot and heat oil. Add bacon and onion and stir-fry 3–4 minutes until onions are translucent and bacon is almost crisp. Press the Cancel button.
3. Transfer cooked mixture to a greased 7-cup glass bowl and set aside to cool 5 minutes. Pour whisked egg mixture over the cooked mixture and stir to combine.
4. Add water to the Instant Pot and insert steam rack. Place glass bowl with egg mixture on steam rack. Lock lid.
5. Press the Manual or Pressure Cook button and adjust time to 8 minutes. When timer beeps, let pressure release naturally until float valve drops. Unlock lid.
6. Remove bowl from pot and let sit 10 minutes to allow eggs to set. Slice and serve warm.

Western Omelet Casserole

Servings: 4
Cooking Time: 10 Minutes
Ingredients:
- 6 large eggs
- ½ teaspoon sea salt
- ½ teaspoon ground black pepper
- 2 dashes hot sauce
- 1 cup diced ham
- 1 small red bell pepper, seeded and diced
- 1 small green bell pepper, seeded and diced
- 1 small onion, peeled and diced
- 2 cups water

Directions:
1. In a medium bowl, whisk together eggs, salt, pepper, and hot sauce. Set aside.
2. Press the Sauté button on Instant Pot. Stir-fry ham, bell peppers, and onion for 3–5 minutes or until onions are translucent.
3. Transfer mixture to a greased 7-cup glass dish. Pour whisked eggs over the ham mixture.
4. Place trivet in Instant Pot. Pour in water. Place dish with egg mixture onto trivet. Lock lid.
5. Press the Manual button and adjust time to 5 minutes. When timer beeps, quick-release pressure until float valve drops and then unlock lid.

6. Remove dish from the Instant Pot. Let sit at room temperature for 5–10 minutes to allow the eggs to set. Slice and serve.

Banana & Vanilla Pancakes

Servings: 6
Cooking Time: 15 Minutes
Ingredients:
- 2 bananas, mashed
- 1 ¼ cups milk
- 2 eggs
- 1 ½ cups rolled oats
- 1 ½ tsp baking powder
- 1 tsp vanilla extract
- 2 tsp coconut oil
- 1 tbsp honey

Directions:
1. Combine the bananas, milk, eggs, oats, baking powder, vanilla, coconut oil, and honey in a blender and pulse until a completely smooth batter. Grease the inner pot with cooking spray. Spread 1 spoon batter at the bottom. Cook for 2 minutes on Sauté, flip the crepe, and cook for another minute. Repeat the process with the remaining batter. Serve immediately with your favorite topping.

Tofu Hash Brown Breakfast

Servings: 4
Cooking Time: 21 Minutes
Ingredients:
- 1 cup tofu cubes
- 2 cups frozen hash browns
- 8 beaten eggs
- 1 cup shredded cheddar
- ¼ cup milk
- Salt and pepper to taste

Directions:
1. Set your Instant Pot to Sauté. Place in tofu and cook until browned on all sides, about 4 minutes. Add in hash brown and cook for 2 minutes. Beat eggs, cheddar cheese, milk, salt, and pepper in a bowl and pour over hash brown. Seal the lid, select Manual, and cook for 5 minutes on High. Once done, perform a quick pressure release. Cut into slices before serving.

Cinnamon Roll Doughnut Holes

Servings: 14
Cooking Time: 16 Minutes
Ingredients:
- 1 package Krusteaz Cinnamon Roll Supreme Mix (includes icing packet)
- 6 tablespoons unsalted butter, melted
- ½ cup cold water
- ¼ cup chopped pecans
- 1 cup water

Directions:
1. In a medium bowl, combine dry mix, butter, and ½ cup cold water. Fold in pecans. Spoon half of batter into a greased seven-hole silicone egg mold. If your egg mold has a silicone top, use this. If your egg mold came with a plastic top, do not use. Instead, cover with aluminum foil.
2. Add 1 cup water to the Instant Pot and insert steam rack. Place egg mold on steam rack. Lock lid.
3. Press the Manual or Pressure Cook button and adjust time to 8 minutes. When timer beeps, quick-release pressure until float valve drops. Unlock lid.
4. Pop doughnut holes out of egg mold and repeat with remaining batter.
5. When doughnut holes are cooled, mix icing packet with 1 ½ tablespoons water and dip doughnut holes into glaze to cover. Serve.

Sausage And Sweet Potato Hash

Servings: 4
Cooking Time: 10 Minutes
Ingredients:
- ½ pound ground pork sausage
- 1 large sweet potato, peeled and grated
- 1 small yellow onion, peeled and diced
- 2 cloves garlic, peeled and minced
- 1 medium green bell pepper, seeded and diced
- 1 tablespoon Italian seasoning
- ½ teaspoon salt
- ½ teaspoon ground black pepper
- 2 cups water

Directions:
1. Press the Sauté button on the Instant Pot. Stir-fry sausage, sweet potato, onion, garlic, bell pepper, Italian seasoning, salt, and black pepper 3–5 minutes until onions are translucent. Press the Cancel button.
2. Transfer mixture to a greased 7-cup glass baking dish.
3. Add water to the Instant Pot and insert steam rack. Place dish on steam rack. Lock lid.

4. Press the Manual or Pressure Cook button and adjust time to 5 minutes. When timer beeps, quick-release pressure until float valve drops. Unlock lid.
5. Remove dish from the Instant Pot. Spoon hash onto plates and serve.

Egg Muffins To Go

Servings:3
Cooking Time: 15 Minutes
Ingredients:
- 1 tablespoon olive oil
- 3 pieces bacon, diced
- 1 small onion, peeled and diced
- 4 large eggs
- 2 teaspoons Italian seasoning
- ½ teaspoon sea salt
- ½ teaspoon ground black pepper
- ¼ cup shredded Cheddar cheese
- 1 small Roma tomato, diced
- ¼ cup chopped spinach
- 1 cup water

Directions:
1. Press the Sauté button on Instant Pot. Heat olive oil. Add bacon and onion and stir-fry 3–5 minutes until onions are translucent. Transfer mixture to a small bowl to cool.
2. In a medium bowl, whisk together eggs, Italian seasoning, salt, black pepper, cheese, tomatoes, and spinach. Stir in cooled bacon mixture.
3. Place trivet into Instant Pot. Pour in water. Place steamer basket on trivet.
4. Distribute egg mixture evenly among 6 silicone muffin cups. Carefully place cups on steamer basket. Lock lid.
5. Press the Manual button and adjust time to 8 minutes. When the timer beeps, quick-release pressure until float valve drops and then unlock lid.
6. Remove egg muffins and serve warm.

Pumpkin Steel Cut Oats With Cinnamon

Servings: 4
Cooking Time: 25 Minutes
Ingredients:
- 1 tbsp butter
- 2 cups steel-cut oats
- ¼ tsp cinnamon
- 1 cup pumpkin puree
- 3 tbsp maple syrup
- 2 tsp pumpkin seeds, toasted

Directions:
1. Melt butter on Sauté. Add in cinnamon, oats, pumpkin puree, and 3 cups of water. Seal the lid, select Porridge and cook for 10 minutes on High Pressure to get a few bite oats or for 14 minutes to form soft oats. Do a quick release. Open the lid and stir in maple syrup. Top with pumpkin seeds and serve.

Banana Nut Bread Oatmeal

Servings:2
Cooking Time: 7 Minutes
Ingredients:
- 1 cup old-fashioned oats
- 1 cup water
- 1 cup whole milk
- 2 ripe bananas, peeled and sliced
- 2 tablespoons pure maple syrup
- 2 teaspoons ground cinnamon
- ¼ teaspoon vanilla extract
- 2 tablespoons chopped walnuts
- Pinch of salt

Directions:
1. In the Instant Pot bowl, add the oats, water, milk, bananas, maple syrup, cinnamon, vanilla, walnuts, and salt. Stir to combine. Lock lid.
2. Press the Manual button and adjust time to 7 minutes. When the timer beeps, let pressure release naturally until float valve drops and then unlock lid.
3. Stir oatmeal. Spoon the cooked oats into two bowls. Serve warm.

Savory Roast Beef Sandwiches

Servings: 8
Cooking Time: 1 Hour 30 Minutes
Ingredients:
- 2 ½ lb beef roast
- 2 tbsp olive oil
- 1 onion, chopped
- 4 garlic cloves, minced
- ½ cup dry red wine
- 2 cups beef broth stock
- 16 slices Fontina cheese

- 8 split hoagie rolls
- Salt and pepper to taste

Directions:

1. Season the beef with salt and pepper. Warm oil on Sauté and brown the beef for 2 to 3 minutes per side; reserve. Add onion and garlic to the pot and cook for 3 minutes until translucent. Set aside. Add red wine to deglaze. Mix in beef broth and take back the beef. Seal the lid and cook on High Pressure for 50 minutes. Release the pressure naturally for 10 minutes. Preheat a broiler.

2. Transfer the beef to a cutting board and slice. Roll the meat and top with onion. Each sandwich should be topped with 2 Fontina cheese slices. Place the sandwiches under the broiler for 2-3 minutes until the cheese melts.

Tex-mex Breakfast

Servings:4
Cooking Time: 10 Minutes

Ingredients:

- 6 large eggs
- ½ teaspoon sea salt
- ¼ teaspoon ground black pepper
- ⅛ teaspoon chili powder
- ½ cup shredded Cheddar cheese
- 1 small Roma tomato, diced
- 2 tablespoons butter
- 2 small Yukon gold potatoes, grated
- 2 cups cubed cooked ham
- 1 small onion, peeled and diced
- 1 small jalapeño, seeded and diced
- ½ cup sliced button mushrooms
- 2 cups water

Directions:

1. In a medium bowl, whisk together eggs, salt, pepper, and chili powder. Stir in cheese and tomato. Set aside.

2. Press the Sauté button on Instant Pot. Heat the butter and stir-fry potatoes, ham, onion, jalapeño, and mushrooms for approximately 5 minutes until the potatoes are tender and onions are translucent.

3. Transfer cooked mixture to a 7-cup greased glass dish. Pour whisked eggs over the potato mixture.

4. Place trivet in Instant Pot. Pour in water. Place dish with egg mixture onto trivet. Lock lid.

5. Press the Manual button and adjust time to 5 minutes. When timer beeps, quick-release pressure until float valve drops and then unlock lid.

6. Remove dish from the Instant Pot. Let sit at room temperature for 5–10 minutes to allow the eggs to set. Slice and serve warm.

Hard-"boiled" Eggs

Servings:6
Cooking Time: 6 Minutes

Ingredients:

- 1 cup water
- 6 large eggs

Directions:

1. Add water to the Instant Pot and insert steamer basket. Place eggs in basket. Lock lid.

2. Press the Manual or Pressure Cook button and adjust time to 6 minutes. When timer beeps, quick-release pressure until float valve drops. Unlock lid.

3. Create an ice bath by adding 1 cup ice and 1 cup water to a medium bowl. Transfer eggs to ice bath to stop the cooking process.

4. Peel eggs. Slice each egg directly onto a plate. Serve immediately.

Crustless Crab Quiche

Servings:6
Cooking Time: 10 Minutes

Ingredients:

- 6 large eggs
- ¼ cup unsweetened almond milk
- 2 teaspoons fresh thyme leaves
- ½ teaspoon sea salt
- ¼ teaspoon ground black pepper
- ½ teaspoon hot sauce
- ½ pound crabmeat
- ¼ cup crumbled goat cheese
- 2 thick slices bacon, diced
- ¼ cup peeled and diced onion
- ¼ cup seeded and diced green bell pepper
- 2 cups water

Directions:

1. In a medium bowl, whisk eggs, milk, thyme leaves, salt, pepper, and hot sauce. Stir in crabmeat and goat cheese. Set aside.

2. Grease a 7-cup glass dish. Set aside.

3. Press the Sauté button on Instant Pot. Add diced bacon and brown for 2 minutes, rendering some fat. Add onion and bell pepper and stir-fry with bacon until tender.

Transfer mixture to the glass container. Pour in egg mixture.

4. Place trivet in Instant Pot. Pour in water. Place dish with egg mixture onto trivet. Lock lid.

5. Press the Manual button and adjust time to 5 minutes. When timer beeps, let pressure release naturally for 10 minutes. Quick-release any additional pressure until float valve drops and then unlock lid.

6. Remove dish from Instant Pot. Let cool for 10 minutes to allow eggs to set. Slice and serve.

Chicken Sandwiches With Barbecue Sauce

Servings: 4
Cooking Time: 50 Minutes
Ingredients:
- 4 chicken thighs, boneless and skinless
- 2 cups barbecue sauce
- 1 onion, minced
- 2 garlic cloves, minced
- 2 tbsp minced fresh parsley
- 1 tbsp lemon juice
- 1 tbsp mayonnaise
- 2 cups lettuce, shredded
- 4 burger buns

Directions:

1. Into the pot, place the garlic, onion, and barbecue sauce. Add in the chicken and toss it to coat. Seal the lid and cook on High Pressure for 15 minutes. Do a natural release for 10 minutes. Use two forks to shred the chicken and mix it into the sauce. Press Keep Warm and let the mixture simmer for 15 minutes to thicken the sauce until the desired consistency.

2. In a bowl, mix lemon juice, mayonnaise, and parsley; toss lettuce into the mixture to coat. Separate the chicken into equal parts to match the burger buns; top with lettuce and complete the sandwiches.

Blueberry-oat Muffins

Servings: 6
Cooking Time: 9 Minutes
Ingredients:
- 1 cup all-purpose baking flour
- ¼ cup old-fashioned oats
- 2 teaspoons baking powder
- ½ teaspoon baking soda
- ⅛ teaspoon salt
- ½ teaspoon vanilla extract
- 3 tablespoons unsalted butter, melted
- 2 large eggs
- 4 tablespoons granulated sugar
- ⅓ cup blueberries
- 1 cup water

Directions:

1. Grease six silicone cupcake liners.

2. In a large bowl, combine flour, oats, baking powder, baking soda, and salt.

3. In a medium bowl, combine vanilla, butter, eggs, and sugar.

4. Pour wet ingredients from medium bowl into the bowl with dry ingredients. Gently combine ingredients. Do not overmix. Fold in blueberries, then spoon mixture into prepared cupcake liners.

5. Add water to the Instant Pot and insert steam rack. Place cupcake liners on top. Lock lid.

6. Press the Manual or Pressure Cook button and adjust time to 9 minutes. When timer beeps, quick-release pressure until float valve drops. Unlock lid.

7. Remove muffins from pot and set aside to cool 30 minutes. Serve.

Honey Butternut Squash Cake Oatmeal

Servings: 4
Cooking Time: 35 Minutes
Ingredients:
- 3 ½ cups coconut milk
- 1 cup steel-cut oats
- 8 oz butternut squash, grated
- ½ cup sultanas
- 1/3 cup honey
- ¾ tsp ground ginger
- ½ tsp salt
- ½ tsp orange zest
- ¼ tsp ground nutmeg
- ¼ cup walnuts, chopped
- ½ tsp vanilla extract
- ½ tsp sugar

Directions:

1. In the cooker, mix sultanas, orange zest, ginger, milk, honey, butternut squash, salt, oats, and nutmeg. Seal the

lid and cook on High Pressure for 12 minutes. Do a natural release for 10 minutes. Into the oatmeal, stir in the vanilla extract and sugar. Top with walnuts and serve.

Vanilla Chai Latte Oatmeal

Servings: 4
Cooking Time: 35 Minutes
Ingredients:
- 3 ½ cups milk
- ½ cup raw peanuts
- 1 cup steel-cut oats
- ¼ cup agave syrup
- 1 ½ tsp ground ginger
- 1 ¼ tsp ground cinnamon
- ¼ tsp ground allspice
- ¼ tsp ground cardamom
- 1 tsp vanilla extract
- 2 tbsp chopped tea leaves
- ¼ tsp cloves

Directions:
1. With a blender, puree peanuts and milk to obtain a smooth consistency. Transfer into the cooker. To the peanuts mixture, add agave syrup, oats, ginger, allspice, cinnamon, cardamom, tea leaves, and cloves and mix well. Seal the lid and cook on High Pressure for 12 minutes. Let pressure release naturally for 10 minutes. Stir in vanilla and serve.

Pumpkin Spice Latte French Toast Casserole

Servings:4
Cooking Time: 20 Minutes
Ingredients:
- 4 cups cubed whole-wheat bread
- 1½ cups whole milk
- ¼ cup brewed coffee, cooled
- 3 large eggs
- ¼ cup pumpkin purée
- 1 teaspoon vanilla extract
- ¼ cup pure maple syrup
- 2 teaspoons pumpkin pie spice
- Pinch of sea salt
- 3 tablespoons butter, cut into 3 pats
- 1 cup water

Directions:

1. Grease a 7-cup glass dish. Add bread. Set aside.
2. In a medium bowl, whisk together milk, coffee, eggs, pumpkin purée, vanilla, maple syrup, pumpkin pie spice, and salt. Pour over bread; place pats of butter on top.
3. Pour water into Instant Pot. Set trivet in Instant Pot. Place glass dish on top of trivet. Lock lid.
4. Press the Manual button and adjust time to 20 minutes. When the timer beeps, quick-release the pressure until float valve drops and then unlock lid.
5. Remove glass bowl from the Instant Pot. Transfer to a rack until cool. Serve.

Strawberry Jam

Servings: 6
Cooking Time: 30 Minutes
Ingredients:
- 1 lb strawberries, chopped
- 1 cup sugar
- ½ lemon, juiced and zested
- 1 tbsp mint, chopped

Directions:
1. Add the strawberries, sugar, lemon juice, and zest to the Instant Pot. Seal the lid, select manual, and cook for 2 minutes on High.
2. Release pressure naturally for 10 minutes. Open the lid and stir in chopped mint. Select Sauté and continue cooking until the jam thickens, about 10 minutes. Let to cool before serving.

Sweet Potato Morning Hash

Servings:4
Cooking Time: 10 Minutes
Ingredients:
- 6 large eggs
- 1 tablespoon Italian seasoning
- ½ teaspoon sea salt
- ½ teaspoon ground black pepper
- ½ pound ground pork sausage
- 1 large sweet potato, peeled and cubed
- 1 small onion, peeled and diced
- 2 cloves garlic, minced
- 1 medium green bell pepper, seeded and diced
- 2 cups water

Directions:
1. In a medium bowl, whisk together eggs, Italian seasoning, salt, and pepper. Set aside.

2. Press the Sauté button on Instant Pot. Stir-fry sausage, sweet potato, onion, garlic, and bell pepper for 3–5 minutes until onions are translucent.

3. Transfer mixture to a 7-cup greased glass dish. Pour whisked eggs over the sausage mixture.

4. Place trivet in Instant Pot. Pour in water. Place dish with egg mixture onto trivet. Lock lid.

5. Press the Manual button and adjust time to 5 minutes. When timer beeps, quick-release pressure until float valve drops and then unlock lid. Remove dish from Instant Pot. Let sit at room temperature for 5–10 minutes to allow the eggs to set. Slice and serve.

Tomato Mozzarella Basil Egg Bites

Servings:6
Cooking Time: 8 Minutes
Ingredients:
- 4 large eggs
- 2 tablespoons grated yellow onion
- ½ teaspoon salt
- ½ teaspoon ground black pepper
- 6 cherry tomatoes, quartered
- ¼ cup grated mozzarella cheese
- 2 tablespoons chopped fresh basil
- 1 cup water

Directions:
1. Grease six silicone cupcake liners.
2. In a medium bowl, whisk together eggs, onion, salt, and pepper. Distribute egg mixture evenly among cupcake liners. Add tomatoes, cheese, and basil to each cup.
3. Add water to the Instant Pot and insert steam rack. Place steamer basket on steam rack. Carefully place cupcake liners in basket. Lock lid.
4. Press the Manual or Pressure Cook button and adjust time to 8 minutes. When timer beeps, quick-release pressure until float valve drops. Unlock lid.
5. Remove egg bites. Serve warm.

Ham And Swiss Muffin Frittatas

Servings:3
Cooking Time: 15 Minutes
Ingredients:
- 1 tablespoon olive oil
- ¼ cup small-diced ham
- ¼ cup diced red bell pepper, seeded
- 4 large eggs
- ½ teaspoon sea salt
- ½ teaspoon ground black pepper
- ¼ cup shredded Swiss cheese
- 1 cup water

Directions:
1. Press the Sauté button on Instant Pot. Heat olive oil. Add ham and bell pepper and stir-fry 3–5 minutes until peppers are tender. Transfer mixture to a small bowl to cool.
2. In a medium bowl, whisk together eggs, salt, pepper, and Swiss cheese. Stir in cooled ham mixture.
3. Place trivet into Instant Pot. Pour in water. Place steamer basket on trivet.
4. Distribute egg mixture evenly among 6 silicone muffin cups. Carefully place cups on steamer basket. Lock lid.
5. Press the Manual button and adjust time to 8 minutes. When timer beeps, quick-release pressure until float valve drops and then unlock lid.
6. Remove frittatas and serve warm.

California Frittata Bake

Servings:4
Cooking Time: 10 Minutes
Ingredients:
- 4 large eggs
- 4 large egg whites
- ½ teaspoon sea salt
- ¼ teaspoon ground black pepper
- ¼ cup chopped fresh basil
- ½ cup chopped spinach
- 2 small Roma tomatoes, diced
- 1 medium avocado, pitted and diced
- ¼ cup grated Gruyère cheese
- 1 tablespoon avocado oil
- 1 pound ground chicken
- 1 small onion, peeled and diced
- 1 cup water

Directions:
1. In a medium bowl, whisk together eggs, egg whites, salt, and pepper. Add basil, spinach, tomatoes, avocado, and cheese. Set aside.
2. Press the Sauté button on Instant Pot. Heat the avocado oil and stir-fry chicken and onion for

approximately 5 minutes or until chicken is no longer pink.

3. Transfer cooked mixture to a 7-cup greased glass dish and set aside to cool. Once cool pour whisked eggs over the chicken mixture and stir to combine.

4. Place trivet in Instant Pot. Pour in water. Place dish with egg mixture onto trivet. Lock lid.

5. Press the Manual button and adjust time to 5 minutes. When the timer beeps, let pressure release naturally until the float valve drops and then unlock the lid.

6. Remove dish from the Instant Pot and set aside for 5–10 minutes to allow the eggs to set. Slice and serve.

Speedy Soft-boiled Eggs

Servings: 4
Cooking Time: 10 Minutes
Ingredients:
- 4 large eggs
- Salt and pepper to taste

Directions:
1. To the pressure cooker, add 1 cup of water and place a wire rack. Place eggs on it. Seal the lid, press Steam, and cook for 3 minutes on High Pressure. Do a quick release.

2. Allow to cool in an ice bath. Peel the eggs and season with salt and pepper before serving.

Greek Yogurt With Honey & Walnuts

Servings: 10
Cooking Time: 15hr
Ingredients:
- 2 tbsp Greek yogurt
- 8 cups milk
- ¼ cup sugar honey
- 1 tsp vanilla extract
- 1 cup walnuts, chopped

Directions:
1. Add the milk to your Instant Pot. Seal the lid and press Yogurt until the display shows "Boil". When the cooking cycle is over, the display will show Yogurt. Open the lid and check that milk temperature is at least 175°F. Get rid of the skin lying on the milk's surface. Let cool in an ice bath until it becomes warm to the touch.

2. In a bowl, mix one cup of milk and yogurt to make a smooth consistency. Mix the milk with yogurt mixture. Transfer to the pot and place on your Pressure cooker.

3. Seal the lid, press Yogurt, and adjust the timer to 9 hrs. Once cooking is complete, strain the yogurt into a bowl using a strainer with cheesecloth. Chill for 4 hours.

4. Add in vanilla and honey and gently stir well. Spoon the yogurt into glass jars. Serve sprinkled with walnuts and enjoy.

Bacon Cheddar Scrambled Egg Muffins

Servings:6
Cooking Time: 8 Minutes
Ingredients:
- 4 large eggs
- 2 tablespoons whole milk
- 2 tablespoons grated yellow onion
- ½ teaspoon salt
- ½ teaspoon ground black pepper
- 5 slices bacon, cooked and crumbled
- ¼ cup grated Cheddar cheese
- 1 cup water

Directions:
1. Grease six silicone cupcake liners.

2. In a medium bowl, whisk together eggs, milk, onion, salt, and pepper. Distribute egg mixture evenly among cupcake liners. Add equal amounts of bacon and cheese to each cup.

3. Add water to the Instant Pot and insert steam rack. Place steamer basket on steam rack. Carefully place muffin cups in basket. Lock lid.

4. Press the Manual or Pressure Cook button and adjust time to 8 minutes. When timer beeps, quick-release pressure until float valve drops. Unlock lid.

5. Remove egg muffins. Serve warm.

Breakfast Frittata

Servings: 4
Cooking Time: 25 Minutes
Ingredients:
- 8 beaten eggs
- 1 cup cherry tomatoes, halved
- 1 tbsp Dijon mustard
- 1 cup mushrooms, chopped
- Salt and pepper to taste
- 1 cup sharp cheddar, grated

Directions:

1. Combine the eggs, mushrooms, mustard, salt, pepper, and ½ cup of cheddar cheese in a bowl. Pour in a greased baking pan and top with the remaining cheddar cheese and cherry tomatoes. Add 1 cup of water to your Instant Pot and fit in a trivet. Place the baking pan on the trivet.

2. Seal the lid. Select Manual and cook for 15 minutes on High. When ready, perform a quick pressure release and unlock the lid. Slice into wedges before serving.

Trail Mix Oatmeal

Servings:2

Cooking Time: 10 Minutes

Ingredients:
- 1 cup steel-cut oats
- 1½ cups water
- 2 teaspoons butter
- 1 cup freshly squeezed orange juice
- 1 tablespoon dried cranberries
- 1 tablespoon raisins
- 1 tablespoon chopped dried apricots
- 2 tablespoons pure maple syrup
- ¼ teaspoon ground cinnamon
- 2 tablespoons chopped pecans
- Pinch of salt

Directions:

1. Add all ingredients to the Instant Pot bowl and stir to combine. Lock lid.

2. Press the Manual button and adjust time to 10 minutes. When timer beeps, quick-release pressure until float valve drops and then unlock lid.

3. Stir oatmeal. Spoon the cooked oats into two bowls. Serve warm.

Crustless Power Quiche

Servings:2

Cooking Time: 9 Minutes

Ingredients:
- 6 large eggs
- ½ teaspoon salt
- ½ teaspoon ground black pepper
- 2 teaspoons olive oil
- ½ cup diced red onion
- 1 medium red bell pepper, seeded and diced
- ¼ pound ground pork sausage
- 1 ½ cups water
- 1 medium avocado, peeled, pitted, and diced

Directions:

1. In a medium bowl, whisk together eggs, salt, and black pepper. Set aside.

2. Press the Sauté button on the Instant Pot and heat oil. Stir-fry onion, bell pepper, and sausage 3–4 minutes until sausage starts to brown and onions are tender. Press the Cancel button.

3. Transfer sausage mixture to a greased 7-cup glass bowl. Pour whisked eggs over the mixture.

4. Add water to the Instant Pot and insert steam rack. Place bowl with egg mixture on steam rack. Lock lid.

5. Press the Manual or Pressure Cook button and adjust time to 5 minutes. When timer beeps, quick-release pressure until float valve drops. Unlock lid.

6. Remove bowl from pot. Let sit at room temperature 5–10 minutes to allow the eggs to set, then remove quiche from bowl, slice, and garnish with avocado. Serve warm.

Peachy Cream Oats

Servings:2

Cooking Time: 7 Minutes

Ingredients:
- 1 cup old-fashioned oats
- 1 cup water
- 1 cup whole milk
- 4 ripe peaches, peeled, pitted, and diced
- 2 tablespoons packed light brown sugar
- ¼ teaspoon vanilla extract
- 2 tablespoons chopped pecans
- Pinch of salt

Directions:

1. In the Instant Pot bowl, add the oats, water, milk, peaches, brown sugar, vanilla, pecans, and salt. Stir to combine. Lock lid.

2. Press the Manual button and adjust time to 7 minutes. When timer beeps, quick-release pressure until float valve drops and then unlock lid.

3. Stir oatmeal. Spoon the cooked oats into two bowls. Serve warm.

Appetizers, Soups & Sides

Delicious Pork & Garbanzo Bean Chili

Servings: 10
Cooking Time: 60 Minutes
Ingredients:
- 1 lb garbanzo beans, soaked overnight
- 1 tbsp olive oil
- 2 onions, finely chopped
- 2 ½ lb ground pork
- 1 jalapeño pepper, minced
- 6 garlic cloves, minced
- ¼ cup chili powder
- 2 tbsp ground cumin
- Salt to taste
- 1 tsp smoked paprika
- 1 tsp dried oregano
- 1 tsp garlic powder
- ¼ tsp cayenne pepper
- 2 ½ cups beef broth
- 1 tbsp tomato puree

Directions:
1. Add the beans and pour in cold water to cover 1 inch. Seal the lid and cook for 20 minutes on High Pressure. Release the pressure quickly. Drain beans and rinse with cold water. Set aside. Wipe clean the pot and set to Sauté. Warm olive oil, add the onions and sauté for 3 minutes until soft. Add jalapeño, pork, and garlic, and stir-fry until it is cooked through, about 5 minutes.
2. Stir in chili powder, salt, garlic powder, paprika, cumin, oregano, and cayenne, and cook until soft, about 30 seconds. Pour in broth, beans, and tomato puree. Seal the lid and cook for 20 minutes on High Pressure. Release the pressure naturally. Open the lid, press Sauté, and cook as you stir until desired consistency is attained. Spoon chili into bowls and serve.

Cauliflower & Potato Soup With Parsley

Servings: 4
Cooking Time: 30 Minutes
Ingredients:
- 1 lb cauliflower florets
- 2 potatoes, chopped
- 4 cups chicken broth
- 2 tbsp parsley, chopped
- Salt and pepper to taste
- ¼ cup heavy cream
- ¼ cup sour cream
- 1 cup milk

Directions:
1. Add cauliflower, potatoes, broth, parsley, salt, pepper, heavy cream, sour cream, and milk to the pot. Seal the lid and set the steam release handle. Cook on High Pressure for 20 minutes. Do a quick release. Let chill and transfer to a blender. Pulse until well-combined. Serve.

Crushed Potatoes With Aioli

Servings: 4
Cooking Time: 25 Minutes
Ingredients:
- 1 lb Russet potatoes, pierced
- Salt and pepper to taste
- 2 tbsp olive oil
- 4 tbsp mayonnaise
- 1 tsp garlic paste
- 1 tbsp lemon juice

Directions:
1. Mix the olive oil, salt, and pepper in a bowl. Add in the potatoes and toss to coat. Pour 1 cup of water into your Instant Pot and fit in a trivet. Place the potatoes on the trivet and seal the lid. Select Manual and cook for 12 minutes on High. Once ready, perform a quick release.
2. In a small bowl, combine the mayonnaise, garlic paste, and lemon juice and whisk well. Peel and crush the potatoes and transfer to a serving bowl. Serve with aioli.

Chorizo Soup With Roasted Tomatoes

Servings: 6
Cooking Time: 25 Minutes
Ingredients:
- 28 oz fire-roasted diced tomatoes
- 3 tbsp olive oil
- 2 shallots, chopped
- 3 cloves garlic, minced

- Salt and pepper to taste
- 4 cups beef broth
- ½ cup tomatoes, chopped
- ½ cup raw cashews
- 1 tbsp red wine vinegar
- 3 chorizo sausage, chopped
- ½ cup chopped basil

Directions:
1. Warm oil on Sauté and cook chorizo until crispy. Remove to a plate lined with paper towels. Add in garlic and shallots and cook for 5 minutes until soft. Season with salt. Stir in red wine vinegar, broth, fire-roasted tomatoes, cashews, tomatoes, and pepper into the cooker. Seal the lid and cook on High Pressure for 8 minutes. Release the pressure quickly. Pour the soup into a blender and process until smooth. Divide into bowls. Top with chorizo and decorate with basil.

Tangy Egg Snacks

Servings: 6
Cooking Time: 14 Minutes
Ingredients:
- ¼ tsp onion powder
- 6 eggs
- ½ tsp chili powder
- ¼ tsp sea salt
- ¼ tsp garlic powder
- Salt and black pepper to taste

Directions:
1. Grease a baking dish with cooking spray, crack the eggs, and whisk them. Sprinkle with salt, pepper, onion powder, chili powder, and garlic powder. Pour in 1 cup of water in your Instant Pot and fit in a trivet. Place the dish on the trivet and seal the lid. Select Manual and cook for 4 minutes on High pressure. When done, perform a quick pressure release and unlock the lid. Remove onto a cutting board and slice into cubes before serving.

Savory Butternut Squash Soup

Servings: 6
Cooking Time: 25 Minutes
Ingredients:
- 1 tablespoon olive oil
- 1 small onion, peeled and diced
- 2 celery stalks, sliced
- 3 pounds butternut squash, peeled, seeded, and cubed
- 1 small Granny Smith apple, peeled, cored, and diced
- 1 teaspoon sea salt
- ¼ teaspoon white pepper
- 1 teaspoon celery seed
- ¼ teaspoon ground nutmeg
- ¼ teaspoon hot sauce
- 1" piece of fresh ginger, peeled and minced
- 4 cups chicken broth

Directions:
1. Press the Sauté button on the Instant Pot and heat the oil. Add the onion and celery. Sauté for 5 minutes until onions are translucent. Add the butternut squash and apple. Continue to sauté for 2–3 minutes until apples are tender. Add remaining ingredients. Lock lid.
2. Press the Manual button and adjust time to 15 minutes. When timer beeps, quick-release pressure until float valve drops and then unlock lid.
3. In the Instant Pot, purée soup with an immersion blender, or use a stand blender and purée in batches. Ladle into bowls and serve warm.

Frittata With Vegetables & Cheese

Servings: 4
Cooking Time: 30 Minutes
Ingredients:
- 4 eggs
- 8 oz spinach, finely chopped
- ½ cup cheddar, shredded
- ½ cup ricotta, crumbled
- 3 cherry tomatoes, halved
- ¼ cup bell pepper, chopped
- 1 cup chopped broccoli
- 4 tbsp olive oil
- Salt and pepper to taste
- ¼ tsp dried oregano
- 2 tsp celery leaves, chopped

Directions:
1. Heat olive oil on Sauté. Add spinach and cook for 5 minutes, stirring occasionally. Add tomatoes, peppers, and broccoli and stir-fry for 3-4 more minutes. In a bowl, Whisk eggs, cheddar cheese, and ricotta cheese. Pour in the pot and cook for 5-7 minutes. Season with salt, black pepper, and oregano; press Cancel. Serve with celery.

Creamy Creamed Corn

Servings: 6
Cooking Time: 7 Minutes
Ingredients:
- 6 large ears of corn or 8 medium, husked
- ½ cup water
- ½ teaspoon sea salt
- ½ teaspoon ground black pepper
- 4 ounces cream cheese, cubed and room temperature
- 4 tablespoons ghee, cubed and room temperature
- 1 teaspoon sugar
- 1 cup heavy cream
- 1 tablespoon flour

Directions:
1. Cut off the corn kernels from the cob, really scraping the cobs to release that milky substance. Place the kernels, water, salt, pepper, cream cheese, ghee, and sugar in the Instant Pot. Lock lid.
2. Press the Manual button and adjust time to 2 minutes.
3. In a small bowl, whisk together the heavy cream and flour to create a slurry.
4. When timer beeps, quick-release the pressure until the float valve drops and then unlock lid. Add the slurry to the corn in the Instant Pot and stir. Press the Keep Warm button and warm unlidded for 5 minutes to thicken.
5. Transfer to a medium bowl and serve warm.

Garlicky Mashed Root Vegetables

Servings: 4
Cooking Time: 5 Minutes
Ingredients:
- 2 medium turnips, peeled and diced
- 2 medium parsnips, peeled and diced
- 1 large Yukon gold potato, peeled and diced
- 3 cloves garlic, peeled and halved
- 1 medium shallot, peeled and quartered
- ½ cup chicken broth
- 1 cup water
- ¼ cup unsweetened almond milk
- 2 tablespoons ghee
- ½ teaspoon sea salt
- ½ teaspoon ground black pepper

Directions:
1. Add the turnips, parsnips, potato, garlic, shallot, broth, and water to Instant Pot. Lock lid.
2. Press the Manual button and adjust time to 5 minutes. When timer beeps, let pressure release naturally for 10 minutes. Quick-release any additional pressure until the float valve drops and then unlock lid.
3. Transfer vegetables to a medium bowl. Add milk, ghee, salt, and pepper. Using a hand-held mixer or immersion blender, purée mixture until smooth. Add additional broth 1 tablespoon at a time from the Instant Pot if mixture is too thick. Serve warm.

Twice-baked Potatoes

Servings: 4
Cooking Time: 13 Minutes
Ingredients:
- 1 cup water
- 2 medium russet potatoes
- 2 slices bacon, cooked and crumbled
- ¼ cup whole milk
- 4 tablespoons unsalted butter
- ½ cup shredded Cheddar cheese, divided
- ½ teaspoon salt
- ¼ teaspoon ground black pepper

Directions:
1. Add water to the Instant Pot and insert steamer basket. Pierce potatoes with a fork and add to basket. Lock lid.
2. Press the Manual or Pressure Cook button and adjust time to 10 minutes. When timer beeps, let pressure release naturally until float valve drops. Press the Cancel button. Unlock lid.
3. Transfer potatoes to a cutting board and let cool enough to handle.
4. In a medium mixing bowl, add bacon, milk, butter, ¼ cup cheese, salt and pepper.
5. Slice potatoes in half lengthwise. Scoop out potato flesh, leaving a bowl-like shell.
6. Add scooped potatoes to bowl with remaining ingredients. Using a potato masher or the back of a fork, work ingredients together. Distribute mixture evenly among the bowl-like shells. Sprinkle with remaining cheese. Place potatoes in basket and insert in the Instant Pot. Lock lid.
7. Press the Manual or Pressure Cook button and adjust time to 3 minutes. When timer beeps, let pressure release naturally until float valve drops. Unlock lid. Serve.

Pork Ribs With Onions

Servings: 4
Cooking Time: 35 Minutes
Ingredients:
- 1 ½ cups tomato puree
- 1 tbsp garlic, minced
- Salt and pepper to taste
- 1 ¼ cups sweet onions
- ½ cup carrots, thinly sliced
- 1 lb cut pork spare ribs

Directions:
1. Brown the ribs on Sauté. Pour in 1 ½ cups water and tomato puree. Add garlic, salt, pepper, onions, and carrots. Seal the lid and cook for 30 minutes on Pressure Cook on High. Once ready, do a quick pressure release and serve.

Chili Corn On The Cob

Servings: 4
Cooking Time: 10 Minutes
Ingredients:
- 4 ears corn on the cob, husked
- 1 Poblano chili pepper, chopped
- 4 tbsp butter, softened
- 2 tbsp parsley, chopped

Directions:
1. Pour 1 cup of water into your Instant Pot and fit in a trivet. Mix the chili pepper, parsley, and butter in a blender until smooth. Rub the mixture all over the corn and place on the trivet. Seal the lid, select Manual, and cook for 2 minutes on High pressure. Serve right away.

Happy Dip

Servings: 8
Cooking Time: 3 Minutes
Ingredients:
- 8 ounces cream cheese, softened
- 1 tablespoon Italian seasoning
- 6 slices bacon, cooked and crumbled
- 2 cups shredded sharp Cheddar cheese
- 16 ounces sour cream
- 1 medium green onion, sliced (whites and greens separated)
- 1 cup water

Directions:
1. In a medium bowl, combine cream cheese, Italian seasoning, bacon, Cheddar cheese, sour cream, and onion whites. Transfer mixture to a 7-cup glass bowl.
2. Add water to the Instant Pot and insert steam rack. Place glass bowl on steam rack. Lock lid.
3. Press the Manual or Pressure Cook button and adjust time to 3 minutes. When timer beeps, quick-release pressure until float valve drops. Unlock lid.
4. Remove glass baking dish from pot. Garnish with onion greens. Serve warm.

Sumac Red Potatoes

Servings: 4
Cooking Time: 16 Minutes
Ingredients:
- 2 tbsp butter
- 1 lb red potatoes wedges
- 2 tbsp sumac
- Salt and pepper to taste

Directions:
1. Melt the butter in your Instant Pot on Sauté. Mix the potatoes, sumac, and ½ cup of water and seal the lid. Select Manual and cook for 6 minutes on High pressure. Once ready, perform a quick pressure release and unlock the lid. Sprinkle with salt and pepper. Serve immediately.

Vegetarian Soup With White Beans

Servings: 4
Cooking Time: 30 Minutes
Ingredients:
- 1 cup green peas
- 1 carrot, chopped
- 2 red bell peppers, chopped
- ½ cup white beans, soaked
- 1 tomato, roughly chopped
- 4 cups vegetable broth
- 1 onion, chopped
- 2 tbsp olive oil
- Salt and pepper to taste
- ¼ tsp dried oregano

Directions:
1. Heat the olive oil on Sauté and stir-fry onion, carrot, and bell peppers for 5 minutes until tender. Stir in green peas, white beans, tomato, broth, salt, pepper, and oregano. Seal the lid. Cook on High Pressure for 20 minutes. Do a quick release. Serve warm.

Spicy Chicken Chili

Servings: 8
Cooking Time: 40 Minutes
Ingredients:

- 1 tablespoon olive oil
- 1 pound ground chicken
- 1 medium yellow onion, peeled and diced
- 3 cloves garlic, minced
- 3 canned chipotle chilies in adobo sauce
- 1 can dark red kidney beans, drained and rinsed
- 1 can black beans, drained and rinsed
- 1 teaspoon Worcestershire sauce
- 1 can diced tomatoes, including liquid
- 1 can diced green chilies, including liquid
- 1 teaspoon sea salt
- 2 teaspoons hot sauce
- 1 teaspoon smoked paprika
- 1 teaspoon chili powder

Directions:
1. Press the Sauté button on the Instant Pot. Heat oil. Add the ground chicken and onion and stir-fry approximately 5 minutes until chicken is no longer pink.
2. Stir in the remaining ingredients. Lock lid.
3. Press the Meat button and cook for the default time of 35 minutes.
4. When timer beeps, let pressure release naturally until float valve drops and then unlock lid.
5. Ladle into individual bowls and serve warm.

Italian-style Brussels Sprouts

Servings: 4
Cooking Time: 15 Minutes
Ingredients:

- 1 lb Brussels sprouts, halved
- 2 garlic cloves, minced
- 1 tbsp mustard seeds
- 1 cup vegetable broth
- Salt and pepper to taste
- 1 tsp olive oil
- 2 tbsp rosemary, chopped

Directions:
1. Heat the olive oil in your Instant Pot and on Sauté. Cook Brussels sprouts, garlic, and mustard seeds for 2 minutes, stirring often. Pour in vegetable broth, salt, and pepper and seal the lid. Select Manual and cook for 4 minutes on High pressure. When done, perform a quick pressure release and unlock the lid. Serve topped with rosemary.

Goat Cheese & Beef Steak Salad

Servings: 4
Cooking Time: 55 Minutes
Ingredients:

- 1 lb rib-eye steak, boneless
- 4 oz fresh arugula
- 1 large tomato, sliced
- ¼ cup fresh goat's cheese
- 4 almonds, chopped
- 4 walnuts, chopped
- 4 hazelnuts
- 3 tbsp olive oil
- 2 cups beef broth
- 2 tbsp red wine vinegar
- 1 tbsp Italian seasoning

Directions:
1. In a bowl, whisk the red wine vinegar, Italian seasoning, and olive oil. Brush each steak with the mixture and place it in your Instant Pot. Pour in the broth and seal the lid. Cook on Meat/Stew for 25 minutes on High. Release the pressure naturally for 10 minutes. Unlock the lid. Remove the steaks along with the broth. Grease the inner pot with oil and hit Sauté. Brown the steaks on both sides for 5-6 minutes. Remove from the pot and chill for 5 minutes before slicing. In a bowl, mix arugula, tomato, cheese, almonds, walnuts, and hazelnuts. Top with steaks and drizzle with red wine mixture. Serve.

Homemade Vichyssoise Soup With Chives

Servings: 4
Cooking Time: 30 Minutes
Ingredients:

- 2 tbsp butter
- 3 leeks, chopped
- 2 cloves garlic, minced
- 4 cups vegetable broth
- 3 potatoes, peeled, cubed
- ½ cup sour cream
- 2 tbsp rosemary
- Salt and pepper to taste
- 2 tbsp chives, chopped

Directions:

1. Melt butter on Sauté. Stir in garlic and leeks and cook for 3-4 minutes until soft. Stir in potatoes, rosemary, and broth. Seal the lid and cook on High Pressure for 15 minutes. Release pressure quickly. Transfer soup to a food processor and puree to obtain a smooth consistency. Season with salt and pepper. Top with fresh chives and sour cream. Serve

Pea & Beef Stew

Servings: 6
Cooking Time: 35 Minutes
Ingredients:
- 1 cup mixed wild mushrooms
- 1 cup green peas
- 1 cup diced potatoes
- 1 lb cubed beef
- 3 sliced carrots
- 1 tsp red pepper flakes
- 2 sliced garlic cloves
- ½ cup dry red wine
- 2 tbsp butter
- 1 diced onion
- 2 cups beef broth
- 14 oz can diced tomatoes

Directions:

1. Melt the butter in your Instant Pot on Sauté. Place the onion and cook for 3 minutes until soft. Add in beef cubes and cook for 5-7 minutes until the meat browns. Add in garlic and cook for 1 minute until fragrant. Pour in red wine and scrape any brown bits from the bottom.

2. Put in potatoes, carrots, red pepper flakes, mushrooms, beef broth, diced tomatoes, and green peas. Seal the lid, select Manual, and cook for 15 minutes on High pressure. When done, perform a quick pressure release and unlock the lid. Serve immediately.

Asian-style Chicken Soup

Servings: 4
Cooking Time: 35 Minutes
Ingredients:
- 1 tsp soy sauce
- 4 cups chicken broth
- ½ lb chicken breasts, cubed
- 1 tsp cinnamon
- 1 tsp cilantro, chopped
- 1 tbsp olive oil
- 1 tbsp fish sauce
- 1 tsp ginger
- 1 tbsp sugar
- 1 chopped onion
- 2 tsp minced garlic
- Salt and pepper to taste

Directions:

1. Place the olive oil, garlic, and onion in your Instant Pot and cook for 2-3 minutes until soft on Sauté. Stir in chopped chicken, ginger, cilantro, sugar, cinnamon, fish sauce, soy sauce, salt, pepper, and chicken broth. Seal the lid, select Manual, and cook for 15 minutes on High. When done, allow a natural release for 10 minutes. Serve.

Picante Chicken Wings

Servings: 4
Cooking Time: 25 Minutes
Ingredients:
- 2 lb chicken wings
- ¼ cup hot pepper sauce
- 2 tbsp oil
- 4 tbsp butter
- 2 tbsp Worcestershire sauce
- 1 tsp tabasco
- 4 cups chicken broth

Directions:

1. Grease the pot with oil and place the chicken wings. Pour in broth and hot pepper sauce. Seal the lid and cook on Manual for 15 minutes on High. When ready, do a quick release. Unlock the lid Remove the wings and discard the broth. In the pot, melt the butter on Sauté. Brown the wings for 3 minutes, turning once. Add the Worcestershire sauce and tabasco and stir. Serve hot.

Nutty Potatoes

Servings: 4
Cooking Time: 20 Minutes
Ingredients:
- 1 tbsp lemon zest
- Sea salt to taste
- 1 lb baby potatoes
- ¼ cup butter
- ¼ cup honey
- 1 tbsp cornstarch
- 1 cup mixed nuts, chopped

Directions:

1. Mix the potatoes, lemon zest, salt, and 2 cups of of water in your Instant Pot and seal the lid. Select Manual and cook for 10 minutes on High pressure. When done, perform a quick pressure release and unlock the lid. Remove potatoes to a bowl. Melt the butter in the pot on Sauté. Stir in honey, cornstarch, and mixed nuts and cook for 2 minutes. Top the potatoes with sauce to serve.

Steamed Broccoli

Servings:4
Cooking Time: 0 Minutes (it Will Cook While The Pressure Builds)
Ingredients:

- 1 cup water
- 1 medium head broccoli, chopped
- 1 teaspoon lemon juice
- ½ teaspoon sea salt
- 2 teaspoons ghee

Directions:

1. Pour water into Instant Pot. Insert a steamer basket and arrange broccoli on the basket in an even layer. Lock lid.
2. Press the Steam button and adjust time to 0 minutes. The broccoli will steam in the time it takes the pressure to build. When timer beeps, quick-release pressure until float valve drops and then unlock lid.
3. Use retriever tongs to remove steamer basket. Transfer broccoli to a serving dish and toss with lemon juice, salt, and ghee. Serve warm.

Sparerib Nachos

Servings:8
Cooking Time: 40 Minutes
Ingredients:

- 3 pounds pork spareribs, cut into 2-rib sections
- 2 cups beef broth
- 1 packet taco seasoning mix
- 1 bag tortilla chips
- 2 cups shredded Cheddar cheese
- 3 medium Roma tomatoes, diced

Directions:

1. Add ribs, broth, and taco seasoning to the Instant Pot. Lock lid.
2. Press the Manual or Pressure Cook button and adjust time to 40 minutes. When timer beeps, let pressure release naturally for 10 minutes. Quick-release any additional pressure until float valve drops. Unlock lid. When cool enough to handle, use two forks to shred pork off of bones. Discard bones.
3. Scatter chips on a serving platter. Using a slotted spoon, place rib meat over chips. Add cheese and tomatoes. Serve immediately.

Four Cheeses Party Pizza

Servings: 4
Cooking Time: 25 Minutes
Ingredients:

- 1 pizza crust
- ½ cup tomato paste
- 1 tsp dried oregano
- 1 oz cheddar, grated
- 5-6 mozzarella slices
- ¼ cup grated gouda cheese
- ¼ cup grated Parmesan
- 2 tbsp olive oil

Directions:

1. Grease the bottom of a baking dish with 1 tbsp of olive oil. Line some parchment paper. Flour the working surface and roll out the pizza dough to the approximate size of your Instant Pot. Gently fit the dough in the previously prepared baking dish.
2. In a bowl, combine tomato paste with water and dried oregano. Spread the mixture over the dough and finish with cheeses. Add a trivet inside your the pot and Pour in 1 cup of water. Seal the lid, and cook for 15 minutes on High Pressure. Do a quick release. Remove the pizza from the pot using parchment paper. Cut and serve.

Mediterranean Soup With Tortellini

Servings: 4
Cooking Time: 40 Minutes
Ingredients:

- 1 cup cream of mushroom soup
- ½ cup mushrooms, chopped
- 9 oz refrigerated tortellini
- 1 cup green peas
- 2 carrots, chopped
- 2 tbsp olive oil
- 2 shallots, chopped
- 2 garlic cloves, minced
- ½ tsp oregano
- 3 cups vegetable broth

- Salt and pepper to taste
- 2 tbsp Parmesan, shredded

Directions:

1. Heat the olive oil in your Instant Pot on Sauté. Add in shallots and garlic and cook for 3 minutes until translucent. Add in the carrots and mushrooms and continue sautéing for 3-4 minutes. Pour in broth, mushroom soup, and oregano, and tomatoes and seal the lid. Select Manual and cook for 7 minutes on High.

2. Once over, allow a natural release for 10 minutes, then perform a quick pressure release and unlock the lid. Stir in green peas and tortellini and cook for 3-5 minutes on Sauté. Sprinkle with Parmesan cheese and serve.

Chicken & Noodle Soup

Servings: 2
Cooking Time: 35 Minutes
Ingredients:

- 8 oz egg noodles
- 2 Carrots, sliced
- 1 tbsp Olive Oil
- 1 small onion, chopped
- 2 Celery Ribs, diced
- 1 Banana Pepper, minced
- 1 garlic clove, minced
- 1 small Bay Leaf
- 2 Chicken Breasts
- 3 cups Chicken Broth

Directions:

1. Warm olive oil in your Instant Pot on Sauté. Place the onion, celery, carrots, garlic, and banana pepper and cook for 4 minutes. Add in bay leaf, chicken, and broth. Seal the lid, select Manual, and cook for 15 minutes on High. When done, perform a quick pressure release. Transfer the chicken onto a cutting board and shred it. Put the chicken back in the pot with the egg noodles and cook for 7-8 minutes on Sauté. Serve.

Potato & Broccoli Soup With Rosemary

Servings: 4
Cooking Time: 30 Minutes
Ingredients:

- 1 lb broccoli, cut into florets
- 2 potatoes, peeled, chopped
- 4 cups vegetable broth
- ½ tsp dried rosemary
- ½ tsp salt
- ½ cup sour cream

Directions:

1. Place broccoli and potatoes in the pot. Pour the broth, rosemary, and seal the lid. Cook on Soup/Broth for 20 minutes on High. Do a quick release. Carefully unlock the lid and remove the soup to a blender. Pulse to combine. Stir in sour cream and add salt. Serve.

Beanless Chili

Servings:4
Cooking Time: 40 Minutes
Ingredients:

- 1 tablespoon olive oil
- ½ pound ground pork
- ½ pound ground beef
- 1 medium onion, peeled and diced
- 1 small green bell pepper, seeded and diced
- 1 large carrot, peeled and diced
- 3 cloves garlic, minced
- 2 tablespoons chili powder
- 1 teaspoon sea salt
- 2 teaspoons ground black pepper
- 1 small jalapeño, seeded and diced
- 1 can puréed tomatoes (including juice)

Directions:

1. Press the Sauté button on the Instant Pot. Heat oil. Add the ground pork, ground beef, and onion. Stir-fry for 5 minutes until pork is no longer pink.

2. Add remaining ingredients. Lock lid.

3. Press the Meat button and cook for the default time of 35 minutes. When timer beeps, let pressure release naturally until float valve drops and then unlock lid. Serve warm.

Sausage & Egg Casserole

Servings: 4
Cooking Time: 25 Minutes
Ingredients:
- ½ lb smoked sausages, sliced
- 6 beaten eggs
- ½ cup plain yogurt
- 1 cup cheddar, shredded
- ¼ cup chives, chopped
- Salt and pepper to taste

Directions:

1. Beat eggs and yogurt in a bowl. Add in cheddar cheese, smoked sausages, salt, and pepper and mix until combined. Pour 1 cup of water into your Instant Pot and fit in a trivet. Pour egg mixture into a baking dish and place it on top of the trivet. Seal the lid, select Manual, and cook for 15 minutes on High pressure. Once ready, perform a quick pressure release and unlock the lid. Top with chives and serve.

Beans, Rice, & Grains

Risotto With Spring Vegetables & Shrimp

Servings: 4
Cooking Time: 40 Minutes
Ingredients:
- 1 tbsp avocado oil
- 1 lb asparagus, chopped
- 1 cup spinach, chopped
- 1 cup mushrooms, sliced
- 1 cup rice
- 1 ¼ cups chicken broth
- ¾ cup coconut milk
- 1 tbsp coconut oil
- 1 lb shrimp, deveined
- Salt and pepper to taste
- ¾ cup Parmesan, shredded

Directions:
1. Warm the avocado oil on Sauté. Add spinach, mushrooms, and asparagus and sauté for 5 minutes until cooked through. Add in rice, coconut milk, and chicken broth as you stir. Seal the lid, press Manual, and cook for 20 minutes on High Pressure.
2. Do a quick release. Place the rice on a serving plate. Press Sauté. Heat the coconut oil. Add shrimp and cook for 6 minutes until it turns pink. Set the shrimp over rice and season with pepper and salt. Serve topped with Parmesan cheese.

One-pot Mexican Rice

Servings: 4
Cooking Time: 35 Minutes
Ingredients:
- 2 tbsp olive oil
- 1 onion, diced
- 2 garlic cloves, sliced
- 1 cup long-grain white rice
- 2 cups chicken stock
- 1 tbsp chipotle chili paste
- 2 mixed peppers, sliced
- 1 cup salsa
- Salt and pepper to taste
- 2 tbsp cilantro, chopped

Directions:
1. Warm olive oil in your Instant Pot on Sauté and add in onion, garlic, and mixed peppers; cook for 2-3 minutes.
2. Add in rice and cook for another 1-2 minutes. Mix in stock, salsa, salt, and pepper. Seal the lid, select Manual, and cook for 10 minutes on High pressure.
3. When over, allow a natural release for 10 minutes and unlock the lid. Stir in the chipotle paste. Serve topped with cilantro. Enjoy!

Hawaiian Rice

Servings: 4
Cooking Time: 30 Minutes
Ingredients:
- 2 tsp olive oil
- 1 ½ cups coconut water
- 1 cup jasmine rice
- 2 green onions, sliced
- ½ pineapple, and chopped
- Salt to taste
- ¼ tsp red pepper flakes

Directions:
1. Stir olive oil, water, rice, pineapple, and salt in your Instant Pot. Seal the lid, select Manual, and cook for 10 minutes on low pressure. Once over, allow a natural release for 10 minutes, then a quick pressure release. Carefully unlock the lid. Using a fork, fluff the rice. Scatter with green onions and red pepper flakes and serve.

Primavera Egg Noodles

Servings: 4
Cooking Time: 20 Minutes
Ingredients:
- 1 lb asparagus, trimmed
- 2 cups broccoli florets
- 3 tbsp olive oil
- Salt to taste
- 10 oz egg noodles
- 2 garlic cloves, minced
- 2 ½ cups vegetable stock
- ½ cup heavy cream
- 1 cup small tomatoes, halved

- ¼ cup chopped basil
- ½ cup grated Parmesan

Directions:

1. Pour the noodles, vegetable stock, and 2 tbsp olive oil, garlic, and salt in your Instant Pot. Place a trivet over. Combine asparagus, broccoli, remaining olive oil, stock, and salt in a bowl. Place the vegetables on the trivet. Seal the lid. Cook on Manual for 12 minutes.

2. Do a quick release. Remove the vegetables. Stir the heavy cream and tomatoes in the pasta. Press Sauté and simmer the cream for 2 minutes. Mix in asparagus and broccoli. Garnish with basil and Parmesan and serve.

Cranberry Millet Pilaf

Servings: 4
Cooking Time: 20 Minutes

Ingredients:

- ½ cup dried cranberries. chopped
- 2 tbsp olive oil
- 1 garlic clove, minced
- 1 shallot, chopped
- 1 cup long-grain white rice
- 1 cup millet
- Salt and pepper to taste

Directions:

1. Warm olive oil in your Instant Pot on Sauté. Add in shallot and garlic and cook for 3 minutes. Stir in rice, millet, 3 cups water, cranberries, salt, and pepper.

2. Seal the lid and for 10 minutes on Rice. When ready, perform a quick pressure release and unlock the lid. Using a fork, fluff the pilaf. Serve immediately.

Beef Pasta Alla Parmigiana

Servings: 6
Cooking Time: 20 Minutes

Ingredients:

- 3 tsp olive oil
- 1 ¼ lb ground beef
- 1 cup white wine
- 1 tsp onion powder
- 3 beef bouillon cubes
- 1 lb conchiglie pasta shells
- ½ cup Parmesan, shredded
- Salt and pepper to taste
- 5 basil leaves, torn

Directions:

1. Warm olive oil in your Instant Pot on Sauté. Add in the ground beef and stir-fry until browned, about 5 minutes. Place 3 cups of water, onion powder, and bouillon cubes in a bowl and mix to combine. Pour it into the pot. Add in the white wine, pasta, salt, and pepper and seal the lid. Select Manual and cook for 5 minutes on High. Once ready, perform a quick pressure release. Sprinkle with Parmesan cheese and basil and serve.

Quinoa Bowls With Broccoli & Pesto

Servings: 2
Cooking Time: 15 Minutes

Ingredients:

- 1 bunch baby heirloom carrots, peeled
- 1 cup quinoa
- 2 cups vegetable broth
- Salt and pepper to taste
- 1 potato, peeled, cubed
- 10 oz broccoli florets
- ¼ cabbage, chopped
- 2 eggs
- 1 avocado, sliced
- ¼ cup pesto sauce
- Lemon wedges, for serving

Directions:

1. In your Instant Pot, mix the vegetable broth, pepper, quinoa, and salt. Set a trivet on top of the quinoa and place a steamer basket on the trivet. Mix carrots, potato, eggs, and broccoli in the steamer basket. Seal the lid and cook for 1 minute on High Pressure. Quick-release the pressure. Remove the trivet and basket from the pot.

2. Set the eggs in a bowl of ice water. Then peel and halve them. Fluff the quinoa. In two bowls, equally divide avocado, quinoa, broccoli, eggs, carrots, potato, cabbage, and pesto dollop. Serve with lemon wedges.

Cheeseburger Macaroni

Servings:4
Cooking Time: 9 Minutes

Ingredients:

- 1 tablespoon olive oil
- 1 pound 80/20 ground beef
- 1 pound elbow macaroni
- ¼ cup whole milk
- 1 ½ cups shredded sharp Cheddar cheese
- 2 tablespoons unsalted butter

- 2 teaspoons salt
- ½ teaspoon ground black pepper

Directions:

1. Press the Sauté button on the Instant Pot and heat oil. Add ground beef. Stir-fry 5 minutes until browned. Press the Cancel button. Using a slotted spoon, transfer beef to a medium bowl. Set aside. Clean grease from pot.

2. Place macaroni in an even layer in pot. Pour enough water to come about ¼" over pasta. Lock lid.

3. Press the Manual or Pressure Cook button and adjust time to 4 minutes. When timer beeps, let pressure release naturally for 3 minutes. Quick-release any additional pressure until float valve drops. Unlock lid.

4. Drain any residual water. Add milk, cheese, butter, salt, and pepper. Add in cooked ground beef. Stir in the warmed pot until well combined. Serve warm.

Spicy Linguine With Cherry Tomato & Basil

Servings: 4
Cooking Time: 25 Minutes

Ingredients:

- 2 tbsp olive oil
- 1 small onion, diced
- 2 garlic cloves, minced
- 1 cup cherry tomatoes, halved
- 1 ½ cups vegetable stock
- ¼ cup julienned basil leaves
- Salt and pepper to taste
- ¼ tsp red chili flakes
- 1 lb linguine noodles, halved
- 2 tbsp basil leaves
- ½ cup Parmesan, grated

Directions:

1. Warm oil on Sauté. Add onion and Sauté for 2 minutes until soft. Mix garlic and tomatoes and Sauté for 4 minutes. Add vegetable stock, salt, julienned basil, red chili flakes, and pepper to the pot. Add linguine to the tomato mixture until covered. Seal the lid.

2. Cook on High Pressure for 5 minutes. Naturally release the pressure for 10 minutes. Unlock the lid. Divide into plates. Top with basil and Parmesan cheese and serve.

Chicken & Broccoli Rice

Servings: 4
Cooking Time: 40 Minutes

Ingredients:

- 1 red chili, finely chopped
- 2 tbsp butter
- 1 lb chicken breasts, sliced
- 1 onion, chopped
- 2 cloves garlic, minced
- Salt and pepper to taste
- 1 cup long-grain rice
- 2 cups chicken broth
- 10 oz broccoli florets
- 2 tbsp cilantro, chopped

Directions:

1. Melt butter in your Instant Pot on Sauté and add chicken, onion, red chili, garlic, salt, and pepper; cook for 5 minutes, stirring often. Stir in rice, chicken broth, milk, and broccoli. Seal the lid, select Manual, and cook for 15 minutes on High. When ready, allow a natural release for 10 minutes. Sprinkle with cilantro and serve.

Boston Baked Beans

Servings: 10
Cooking Time: 45 Minutes

Ingredients:

- 1 tablespoon olive oil
- 5 slices bacon, diced
- 1 large sweet onion, peeled and diced
- 4 cloves garlic, minced
- 2 cups dried navy beans
- 4 cups chicken broth
- 2 teaspoons ground mustard
- 1 teaspoon sea salt
- ¼ teaspoon ground black pepper
- ¼ cup molasses
- ½ cup ketchup
- ¼ cup packed dark brown sugar
- 1 teaspoon smoked paprika
- 1 teaspoon Worcestershire sauce
- 1 teaspoon apple cider vinegar

Directions:

1. Press Sauté button on Instant Pot. Heat olive oil. Add bacon and onions. Stir-fry for 3–5 minutes until onions are translucent. Add garlic. Cook for an additional minute. Add beans. Toss to combine.

2. Add broth, mustard, salt, and pepper. Lock lid.

3. Press the Bean button and cook for the default time of 30 minutes. When timer beeps, let pressure release naturally for 10 minutes. Quick-release any additional pressure until float valve drops and then unlock lid.

4. Stir in the molasses, ketchup, brown sugar, smoked paprika, Worcestershire sauce, and vinegar. Press the Sauté button on the Instant Pot, press the Adjust button to change the heat to Less, and simmer uncovered for 10 minutes to thicken the sauce; then transfer to a serving dish and serve warm.

Provençal Rice

Servings: 6
Cooking Time: 45 Minutes
Ingredients:
- 2 tbsp butter
- 1 onion, diced
- 2 garlic cloves, minced
- 2 cups brown rice
- 3 cups vegetable stock
- 1 tsp herbs de Provence
- 3 anchovy fillets, finely chopped
- 6 pitted Kalamata olives

Directions:

1. Melt butter in your Instant Pot on Sauté and add in onion and garlic; cook for 3 minutes. Stir in rice and herbs for 1 minute and pour in the stock. Seal the lid, select Manual, and cook for 22 minutes on High. When ready, allow a natural release for 10 minutes and unlock the lid. Stir in anchovy fillets. Serve topped with Kalamata olives.

Garlic Mushroom Polenta

Servings: 4
Cooking Time: 35 Minutes
Ingredients:
- 1 cup mixed mushrooms, sliced
- 2 tsp olive oil
- 4 green onions, chopped
- 2 garlic cloves, sliced
- 2 tbsp cilantro, minced
- 1 tbsp chili powder
- ½ tsp cumin
- Salt and pepper to taste
- ¼ tsp cayenne pepper
- 2 cups veggie stock
- 1 cup polenta

Directions:

1. Warm olive oil in your Instant Pot on Sauté and add mushrooms, garlic, and green onions. Cook for 4 minutes. Stir in chili powder, cumin, salt, pepper, cayenne, and stock. Combine polenta with 1 ½ cups of hot water in a bowl and transfer to the Instant Pot. Seal the lid, select Manual, and cook for 10 minutes on High pressure. Once done, allow a natural release for 10 minutes and unlock the lid. Top with cilantro and serve.

Rice & Chicken Soup

Servings: 4
Cooking Time: 35 Minutes
Ingredients:
- 1 lb chicken breasts, cubed
- 1 carrot, chopped
- 1 onion, chopped
- ¼ cup rice
- 1 potato, finely chopped
- 1 tsp cayenne pepper
- 2 tbsp olive oil
- 4 cups chicken broth

Directions:

1. Heat the olive oil in your Instant Pot on Sauté. Cook the onion, carrot, and chicken for 5 minutes, stirring often. Add in rice, potato, cayenne pepper, and broth and stir. Seal the lid. Cook on Soup/Broth for 20 minutes. Do a quick pressure release. Carefully unlock the lid. Serve.

Rice & Red Bean Pot

Servings: 4
Cooking Time: 55 Minutes
Ingredients:
- 1 cup red beans, soaked
- 2 tbsp vegetable oil
- ½ cup rice
- ½ tbsp cayenne pepper
- 1 ½ cups vegetable broth
- 1 onion, diced
- 1 garlic clove, minced
- 1 red bell pepper, diced
- 1 stalk celery, diced
- Salt and pepper to taste

Directions:

1. Place beans in your Instant Pot with enough water to cover them by a couple of fingers. Seal the lid and cook for 25 minutes on High Pressure. Release the pressure quickly. Drain the beans and set aside.

2. Rinse and pat dry the inner pot. Add in oil and press Sauté. Add in onion and garlic and sauté for 3 minutes until soft. Add celery and bell pepper and cook for 2 minutes.

3. Add in the rice, reserved beans, vegetable broth. Stir in pepper, cayenne pepper, and salt. Seal the lid and cook for 15 minutes on High Pressure. Release the pressure quickly. Carefully unlock the lid. Serve warm.

Parmesan Risotto

Servings: 4
Cooking Time: 20 Minutes
Ingredients:
- 4 tablespoons butter
- 1 small onion, peeled and finely diced
- 2 cloves garlic, minced
- 1½ cups Arborio rice
- 4 cups chicken broth, divided
- 3 tablespoons grated Parmesan cheese
- ½ teaspoon salt
- ¼ teaspoon ground black pepper
- ½ cup chopped fresh parsley

Directions:

1. Press the Sauté button on Instant Pot. Add and melt the butter. Add the onion and stir-fry for 3–5 minutes until onions are translucent. Add garlic and rice and cook for an additional minute. Add 1 cup broth and stir for 2–3 minutes until it is absorbed by the rice.

2. Add remaining 3 cups broth, Parmesan cheese, salt, and pepper. Lock lid.

3. Press the Manual button and adjust time to 10 minutes. When timer beeps, let pressure release naturally for 10 minutes. Quick-release any additional pressure until float valve drops and then unlock lid.

4. Ladle into bowls and garnish each with ⅛ cup fresh parsley.

Basic Basmati White Rice

Servings: 4
Cooking Time: 5 Minutes
Ingredients:
- 2 cups basmati rice
- 1 ¼ cups water
- 1 cup chicken broth
- 1 teaspoon salt
- 1 tablespoon unsalted butter

Directions:

1. Optional step: Some people like to soak their rice in water 1 hour to reduce impurities. If you do this, decrease water added to pot from 1 ¼ cups to 1 cup.

2. Place all ingredients in the Instant Pot. Lock lid.

3. Press the Manual or Pressure Cook button and adjust time to 5 minutes. When timer beeps, let pressure release naturally until float valve drops. Unlock lid.

4. Serve warm.

Mustard Macaroni & Cheese

Servings: 4
Cooking Time: 20 Minutes
Ingredients:
- 16 oz elbow macaroni
- 1 cup heavy cream
- Salt and pepper to taste
- 1 tbsp butter
- 1 tsp mustard powder
- 3 cups cheddar, shredded
- ½ cup Parmesan, grated

Directions:

1. Place macaroni and 4 cups of water in your Instant Pot. Sprinkle with salt and pepper and seal the lid. Select Manual and cook for 4 minutes on High. Once done, perform a quick pressure release. Mix in heavy cream, butter, mustard powder, and cheddar and let sit for 5 minutes. Sprinkle with Parmesan cheese and serve.

Mom's Black-eyed Peas With Garlic & Kale

Servings: 6
Cooking Time: 20 Minutes
Ingredients:
- 1 cup fire-roasted red peppers, diced
- 15 oz can fire-roasted tomatoes
- 1 tsp olive oil
- 1 onion, chopped
- 2 garlic cloves, minced
- ½ tsp ground allspice
- ½ tsp red pepper, crushed
- 1 ½ cups black-eyed peas

- 1 ½ cups vegetable broth
- 2 cups chopped kale

Directions:

1. Warm oil on Sauté. Add onion and garlic and cook for 5 minutes. Season with crushed red pepper, and allspice. Add broth and black-eyed peas to the pot. Seal the lid and cook on High Pressure for 5 minutes. Do a quick pressure release. Mix the peas with kale, red peppers, and tomatoes. Seal the lid and cook on High for 1 minute. Release the pressure quickly. Serve.

Broccoli & Pancetta Carbonara

Servings: 4
Cooking Time: 30 Minutes
Ingredients:
- 1 lb pasta rigatoni
- 12 oz broccoli florets
- ½ fennel bulb, sliced
- 4 large eggs, beaten
- ½ cup Grana Padano, grated
- Salt and pepper to taste
- 8 oz pancetta, chopped
- ¼ cup heavy cream

Directions:

1. Cover the pasta with salted water in your Instant Pot and seal the lid. Select Manual and cook for 4 minutes on High. Drain and set aside, reserving 1 cup of cooking liquid. Beat the eggs in a bowl, add the cheese, and mix to combine. Clean the pot and select Sauté. Cook the pancetta for 4 minutes then add in the fennel; cook for 2-3 more minutes. Pour in the broccoli and pasta liquid and cook for 4-5 minutes. Stir in the egg mixture and heavy cream for 2-3 minutes. Adjust the seasoning. Add the pasta and let sit for 5 minutes before serving.

Asparagus Pasta With Pesto Sauce

Servings: 4
Cooking Time: 15 Minutes
Ingredients:
- 1 cup cherry tomatoes, quartered
- 1 lb farfalle
- 1 lb asparagus, chopped
- ¾ cup pesto sauce
- ½ cup Parmesan, grated

Directions:

1. Place the farfalle and 4 cups of salted water in your Instant Pot and fit in a trivet. Arrange the asparagus on the trivet and seal the lid. Select Manual and cook for 4 minutes on High. Once done, perform a quick pressure release. Drain the pasta and put it back in the pot. Add in the pesto sauce, asparagus, and cherry tomatoes and stir. Sprinkle with Parmesan cheese and serve.

Ziti Green Minestrone

Servings: 4
Cooking Time: 25 Minutes
Ingredients:
- ¼ cup grated Pecorino Romano
- 3 tbsp olive oil
- 1 onion, diced
- 1 celery stalk, diced
- 1 large carrot, diced
- 14 oz can diced tomatoes
- 4 oz ziti pasta
- 1 cup chopped zucchini
- 1 bay leaf
- 1 tbsp mixed herbs
- ¼ tbsp cayenne pepper
- Salt and pepper to taste
- 1 garlic clove, minced
- 1/3 cup olive pesto pasta

Directions:

1. Heat olive oil on Sauté. Cook onion, celery, garlic, and carrot for 3 minutes, stirring occasionally until the vegetables are softened. Stir in ziti, tomatoes, 3 cups water, zucchini, bay leaf, mixed herbs, cayenne, pepper, and salt. Seal the lid and cook on High for 4 minutes.

2. Do a natural pressure release for 10 minutes. Adjust the taste and remove the bay leaf. Ladle the soup into bowls and drizzle the pesto over. Serve topped with Pecorino cheese.

Kiwi Steel Cut Oatmeal

Servings: 4
Cooking Time: 25 Minutes
Ingredients:
- 2 kiwi, mashed
- 2 cups steel cut oatmeal
- ¼ tsp nutmeg
- 1 tsp cinnamon
- 1 tsp vanilla

- ¼ tsp salt
- ½ cup hazelnuts, chopped
- ¼ cup honey

Directions:

1. Place the kiwi, oats, 3 cups water, nutmeg, cinnamon, vanilla, and salt in your Instant Pot and stir to combine. Seal the lid and cook on Manual for 10 minutes on High. When done, allow a natural release for 10 minutes and unlock the lid. Mix in hazelnuts and honey and let chill.

Chickpea & Jalapeño Chicken

Servings: 4
Cooking Time: 40 Minutes

Ingredients:

- 1 lb boneless, skinless chicken legs
- ½ tsp ground cumin
- ½ tsp cayenne pepper
- 2 tbsp olive oil
- 1 onion, minced
- 2 jalapeño peppers, minced
- 3 garlic cloves, crushed
- 2 tbsp freshly grated ginger
- ¼ cup chicken stock
- 24 oz can crushed tomatoes
- 28 oz can chickpeas
- Salt to taste
- ½ cup coconut milk
- ¼ cup parsley, chopped
- 2 cups cooked basmati rice

Directions:

1. Season the chicken with salt, cayenne pepper, and cumin. Set your Instant Pot to Sauté and warm the oil. Add in jalapeño peppers and onion and cook for 5 minutes, stirring occasionally until soft. Mix in ginger and garlic, and cook for 3 minutes until tender. Add ¼ cup chicken stock into the cooker to ensure the pan is deglazed. From the pan's bottom, scrape any browned bits of food.
2. Mix the onion mixture with chickpeas, tomatoes, and salt. Stir in the chicken to coat. Seal the lid and cook on High Pressure for 20 minutes.
3. Release the pressure quickly. Remove the chicken and slice into chunks. Into the remaining sauce, mix coconut milk and simmer for 5 minutes on Sauté. Split rice into 4 bowls. Top with chicken, sauce, and parsley and serve.

Creamed Lentils

Servings: 4
Cooking Time: 20 Minutes

Ingredients:

- 1 tbsp horseradish sauce
- ¼ cup crème fraiche
- 1 cup brown lentils
- 1 cup tomato sauce
- ½ tsp cumin
- Salt to taste
- 1 tsp onion powder
- 1 tsp garlic powder
- 1 tsp chili powder
- 2 tbsp thyme, chopped

Directions:

1. Place 3 cups of water, lentils, tomato sauce, chili powder, garlic powder, onion powder, cumin, and salt in your Instant Pot. Seal the lid, select Manual, and cook for 15 minutes on High pressure. Once ready, perform a quick pressure release and unlock the lid. Stir in horseradish sauce and crème fraiche. Scatter thyme and serve.

Bulgur Pilaf With Roasted Bell Peppers

Servings: 4
Cooking Time: 25 Minutes

Ingredients:

- 2 tbsp olive oil
- 1 garlic clove, minced
- 1 onion, chopped
- 2 cups vegetable stock
- ¼ cup lemon juice
- 1 tsp grated lemon zest
- 1 cup bulgur
- Salt and pepper to taste
- 6 oz roasted bell peppers

Directions:

1. In a bowl, toss bell peppers with some oil, salt, and pepper. Warm the remaining oil on Sauté and cook onion and garlic until soft, about 3 minutes. Stir in stock, lemon juice, lemon zest, and bulgur. Seal the lid and cook on High Pressure for 5 minutes. Do a natural pressure release for 10 minutes. Carefully unlock the lid. Fluff the rice with a fork. Top with roasted peppers to serve.

Weeknight Baked Beans

Servings: 6
Cooking Time: 8 Minutes
Ingredients:
- 2 teaspoons olive oil
- 2 slices bacon, diced
- 1 can great northern beans, drained and rinsed
- 1 can pinto beans, drained and rinsed
- 1 teaspoon salt
- ¼ teaspoon ground black pepper
- ½ cup molasses barbecue sauce
- 1 tablespoon yellow mustard
- 1 cup water

Directions:
1. Line a plate with paper towels.
2. Press the Sauté button on the Instant Pot and heat oil. Add bacon. Stir-fry 3–5 minutes until bacon is almost crisp. Transfer bacon to prepared plate to absorb grease. Press the Cancel button. Rinse pot.
3. In a 7-cup glass baking dish, add bacon, beans, salt, pepper, barbecue sauce, and mustard.
4. Add water to the Instant Pot and insert steam rack. Place glass baking dish on top of steam rack. Lock lid.
5. Press the Manual or Pressure Cook button and adjust time to 3 minutes. When timer beeps, quick-release pressure until float valve drops. Unlock lid.
6. Transfer beans to a bowl. Serve warm.

South American Pot

Servings: 4
Cooking Time: 30 Minutes
Ingredients:
- 1 cups brown rice
- ½ cup soaked black beans
- 1 tbsp tomato paste
- 1 garlic clove, minced
- 2 tsp onion powder
- 2 tsp chili powder
- Salt to taste
- ¼ tsp cumin
- 1 tsp hot paprika
- 3 cups corn kernels

Directions:
1. Place rice, beans, 4 cups water, tomato paste, garlic, onion powder, chili powder, salt, cumin, paprika, and corn in your Instant Pot and stir. Seal the lid, select Manual, and cook for 20 minutes on High pressure. Once ready, perform a quick pressure release and unlock the lid. Adjust the seasoning. Serve immediately.

Cajun Red Beans

Servings: 4
Cooking Time: 40 Minutes
Ingredients:
- 1 tablespoon olive oil
- ½ small yellow onion, peeled and diced
- 1 small red bell pepper, seeded and diced
- 1 medium stalk celery, diced
- 3 cups vegetable broth
- 1 cup (about ½ pound) dried red kidney beans, rinsed and drained
- 1 teaspoon Cajun seasoning
- ½ teaspoon garlic salt
- 2 teaspoons Italian seasoning

Directions:
1. Press the Sauté button on the Instant Pot and heat oil. Add onion, bell pepper, and celery. Stir-fry 3–5 minutes until onions are translucent. Deglaze pot by adding broth and scraping the bottom and sides of pot.
2. Add beans, Cajun seasoning, garlic salt, and Italian seasoning. Press the Cancel button. Lock lid.
3. Press the Manual or Pressure Cook button and cook for 35 minutes. When timer beeps, let pressure release naturally for 10 minutes. Quick-release any additional pressure until float valve drops. Unlock lid.
4. With a slotted spoon, transfer beans to a serving dish. Serve warm.

Honey Coconut Rice

Servings: 4
Cooking Time: 30 Minutes
Ingredients:
- 1 cup Thai sweet rice
- 1 cup coconut milk
- 2 tbsp honey

Directions:
1. Place rice and 1 ½ cups of water in your Instant Pot. Seal the lid, select Manual, and cook for 3 minutes on High pressure. When over, allow a natural release for 10 minutes. Warm coconut milk, and honey in a pot over medium heat until the honey has dissolved. Unlock the lid

of the pressure cooker and stir in coconut mix. Cover with the lid and let sit for 5-10 minutes. Serve.

Lime Brown Rice

Servings: 6
Cooking Time: 45 Minutes
Ingredients:
- ½ bunch spring onions, chopped diagonally
- 2 cups brown rice, rinsed
- 2 small bay leaves
- 2 tbsp olive oil
- 1 lime, juiced
- Salt to taste

Directions:
1. Place the rice, 2 ¾ cups of water, salt, and bay leaves in your Instant Pot. Seal the lid and cook on Manual for 22 minutes on High. When done, allow a natural release for 10 minutes and unlock the lid. Drizzle with olive oil and lime juice and top with spring onions to serve.

Vegan & Vegetarian

Vegan Sloppy Joe's

Servings: 6
Cooking Time: 40 Minutes
Ingredients:
- 3 tbsp olive oil
- 1 chopped onion
- 1 red bell pepper, diced
- 3 cups vegetable broth
- 1 cup green lentils
- 14 oz can diced tomatoes
- 1 tsp chili powder
- 1 tbsp mustard powder
- 1 tbsp brown sugar
- Salt and pepper to taste
- 6 hamburger buns
- 3 dill pickles, sliced

Directions:
1. Warm the olive oil in your Instant Pot. Place in onion and bell pepper and cook for 5 minutes. Stir in vegetable broth, lentils, tomatoes, mustard powder, chili powder, brown sugar, salt, and pepper. Seal the lid, select Manual, and cook for 15 minutes on High pressure. Once over, allow a natural release for 10 minutes and unlock the lid. To assemble, toast each bun and top with lentil mixture and a dill slice. Serve right away.

Cauliflower Rice With Peas & Chili

Servings: 2
Cooking Time: 20 Minutes
Ingredients:
- 10 oz cauliflower florets
- 2 tbsp olive oil
- Salt to taste
- 1 tsp chili powder
- ¼ cup green peas
- 1 tbsp chopped parsley

Directions:
1. Add 1 cup water, set rack over water and place the steamer basket onto the rack. Add cauliflower into the steamer basket. Seal the lid and cook on High Pressure for 1 minute. Release the pressure quickly. Remove rack and steamer basket. Drain water from the pot. Set it to Sauté and warm oil. Add in cauliflower and stir to break into smaller pieces like rice. Stir in chili powder, peas and salt. Serve the cauliflower topped with parsley.

Acorn Squash With Sweet Glaze

Servings: 4
Cooking Time: 15 Minutes
Ingredients:
- 1 lb acorn squash, cut into 2-inch chunks
- 3 tbsp honey
- 2 tbsp butter
- 1 tbsp dark brown sugar
- 1 tbsp cinnamon
- Salt and pepper to taste

Directions:
1. In a small bowl, mix 1 tbsp honey, butter and ½ cup water. Pour into the pot. Add in acorn squash, seal the lid and cook on High Pressure for 4 minutes. Release the pressure quickly. Transfer the squash to a serving dish.
2. Set on Sauté. Mix sugar, cinnamon, the remaining 2 tbsp honey and the liquid in the pot. Cook as you stir for 4 minutes to obtain a thick consistency and turn caramelized and golden. Spread honey glaze over squash; add pepper and salt to taste.

Black Bean Slider Patties

Servings: 8
Cooking Time: 49 Minutes
Ingredients:
- 1 tablespoon olive oil
- 1 small red bell pepper, seeded and diced small
- 2 cups vegetable broth
- 1 cup dried black beans, rinsed and drained
- 2 teaspoons chili powder
- ½ teaspoon salt
- ½ teaspoon ground black pepper
- 1 large egg
- 1 cup panko bread crumbs

Directions:
1. Press the Sauté button on the Instant Pot and heat oil. Add bell pepper and stir-fry 2–3 minutes until pepper is tender. Add broth and deglaze by scraping the bottom and sides of pot.

2. Add beans, chili powder, salt, and pepper. Press the Cancel button. Lock lid.

3. Press the Bean button and cook for the default time of 30 minutes. When timer beeps, let pressure release naturally for 10 minutes. Quick-release any additional pressure until float valve drops. Press the Cancel button. Unlock lid.

4. Press the Sauté button on the Instant Pot, press the Adjust button to change the heat to Less, and simmer bean mixture unlidded 10 minutes to thicken. Transfer mixture to a large bowl.

5. Once bean mixture is cool enough to handle, quickly mix in egg and bread crumbs. Form into sixteen equal-sized small patties.

6. In a medium skillet over medium heat, cook patties approximately 2–3 minutes per side until browned. Serve warm.

Grandma's Asparagus With Feta & Lemon

Servings: 4
Cooking Time: 20 Minutes
Ingredients:
- 1 lb asparagus spears
- 1 tbsp olive oil
- Salt and pepper to taste
- 1 lemon, cut into wedges
- 1 cup feta cheese, cubed

Directions:
1. Into the pot, add 1 cup of water and set trivet over the water. Place steamer basket on the trivet. Place the asparagus into the steamer basket. Seal the lid and cook on High Pressure for 1 minute. Release the Pressure quickly. Add olive oil in a bowl and toss in asparagus until well coated. Season with pepper and salt. Serve with feta and lemon wedges.

Traditional Italian Pesto

Servings: 4
Cooking Time: 20 Minutes
Ingredients:
- 3 zucchini, peeled, chopped
- 1 eggplant, peeled, chopped
- 3 red bell peppers, chopped
- ½ cup basil-tomato juice
- ½ tbsp salt
- 2 tbsp olive oil

Directions:
1. Add zucchini, eggplant, bell peppers, basil-tomato juice, salt, and olive oil to the pot and give it a good stir. Pour 1 cup of water. Seal the lid and cook on High Pressure for 15 minutes. Do a quick release. Set aside to cool completely. Serve as a cold salad or a side dish.

Spicy Split Pea Stew

Servings: 4
Cooking Time: 40 Minutes
Ingredients:
- 2 cups split yellow peas
- 1 cup onion, chopped
- 1 carrot, chopped
- 2 potatoes, chopped
- 2 tbsp butter
- 2 garlic cloves, crushed
- 1 tbsp chili pepper
- 4 cups vegetable stock

Directions:
1. Melt butter on Sauté and stir-fry the onion for 3 minutes. Add peas, carrot, potatoes, and garlic and cook for 5-6 minutes until tender. Stir in chili pepper. Pour in the stock and seal the lid. Cook on Meat/Stew for 25 minutes. Do a quick release. Serve.

Easy Tahini Sweet Potato Mash

Servings: 4
Cooking Time: 15 Minutes
Ingredients:
- 1 cup water
- 2 lb sweet potatoes, cubed
- 2 tbsp tahini
- ¼ tsp ground nutmeg
- 2 tbsp chopped chives
- Salt and pepper to taste

Directions:
1. Into the cooker, add 1 cup water and insert a steamer basket. Put potato cubes into the steamer basket. Seal the lid and cook for 8 minutes at High Pressure. Release the pressure quickly. In a bowl, add cooked sweet potatoes and slightly mash. Using a hand mixer, whip in nutmeg and tahini until the sweet potatoes attain desired consistency. Add salt and pepper and top with chives.

Spicy Shiitake Mushrooms With Potatoes

Servings: 4
Cooking Time: 45 Minutes
Ingredients:
- 1 lb shiitake mushrooms
- 2 potatoes, chopped
- 3 garlic cloves, crushed
- 2 tbsp olive oil
- 1 tsp garlic powder
- 1 tbsp cumin seeds
- ½ tbsp chili powder
- 1 large zucchini, chopped
- 1 cup onions
- 2 cups vegetable stock
- 1 cup tomato sauce

Directions:
1. Warm olive oil on Sauté. Stir-fry cumin seeds for one minute. Add onions, chili powder, garlic, and garlic powder. Cook for 3 minutes, stirring constantly. Add mushrooms and continue to cook on Sauté for 3 more minutes. Add potatoes, zucchini, stock, and tomato sauce and seal the lid. Cook on High Pressure for 20 minutes. When done, release the pressure naturally. Serve warm.

Hot Tofu Meatballs

Servings: 4
Cooking Time: 35 Minutes
Ingredients:
- 1 lb tofu, crumbled
- 2 tbsp butter, melted
- ¼ cup almond meal
- 1 garlic clove, minced
- 2 tbsp olive oil
- 3 tbsp hot sauce
- 2 tbsp chopped scallions
- Salt to taste

Directions:
1. Mix the almond meal, tofu, garlic, salt, and scallions in a bowl. Make meatballs out of the mixture. Warm olive oil in your Instant Pot on Sauté. Place the meatballs and cook for 10 minutes until browned.
2. In the meantime, microwave the butter and hot sauce in a bowl. Combine and set aside. Place the meatballs in the pot and top with hot sauce and 1 cup of water. Seal the lid, select Manual, and cook for 15 minutes on High pressure. When done, perform a quick pressure release and unlock the lid. Serve immediately.

Stuffed Bell Peppers

Servings: 4
Cooking Time: 15 Minutes
Ingredients:
- 4 large bell peppers
- 2 cups cooked white rice
- 1 medium onion, peeled and diced
- 3 small Roma tomatoes, diced
- ¼ cup marinara sauce
- 1 cup corn kernels (cut from the cob is preferred)
- ¼ cup sliced black olives
- ¼ cup canned cannellini beans, rinsed and drained
- ¼ cup canned black beans, rinsed and drained
- 1 teaspoon sea salt
- 1 teaspoon garlic powder
- ½ cup vegetable broth
- 2 tablespoons grated Parmesan cheese

Directions:
1. Cut off the bell pepper tops as close to the tops as possible. Hollow out and discard seeds. Poke a few small holes in the bottom of the peppers to allow drippings to drain.
2. In a medium bowl, combine remaining ingredients except for broth and Parmesan cheese. Stuff equal amounts of mixture into each of the bell peppers.
3. Place trivet into the Instant Pot and pour in the broth. Set the peppers upright on the trivet. Lock lid.
4. Press the Manual button and adjust time to 15 minutes. When timer beeps, let pressure release naturally until float valve drops and then unlock lid.
5. Serve immediately and garnish with Parmesan cheese.

Cannellini Beans With Garlic & Leeks

Servings: 4
Cooking Time: 45 Minutes
Ingredients:
- 1 lb cannellini beans
- 1 onion, chopped
- 2 large leeks, finely chopped
- 3 garlic cloves, whole
- Salt and pepper to taste

- Topping
- 2 tbsp vegetable oil
- 2 tbsp flour
- 1 tbsp cayenne pepper

Directions:
1. Add beans,onion, leeks, garlic, salt, and pepper to the Instant Pot. Press Manual/Pressure Cook and cook for 20 minutes on High. Heat the vegetable oil in a skillet. Add flour and cayenne pepper. Stir-fry for 2 minutes and set aside. When done, do a quick release. Pour in the cayenne mixture and give it a good stir. Let it sit for 15 minutes before serving.

English Vegetable Potage

Servings: 4
Cooking Time: 50 Minutes
Ingredients:
- 1 lb potatoes, cut into bite-sized pieces
- 2 carrots, peeled, chopped
- 3 celery stalks, chopped
- 2 onions, peeled, chopped
- 1 zucchini, sliced
- A handful of celery leaves
- 2 tbsp butter, unsalted
- 3 tbsp olive oil
- 2 cups vegetable broth
- 1 tbsp paprika
- Salt and pepper to taste
- 2 bay leaves

Directions:
1. Warm olive oil on Sauté and stir-fry the onions for 3-4 minutes until translucent. Add carrots, celery, zucchini, and ¼ cup of broth. Continue to cook for 10 more minutes, stirring constantly. Stir in potatoes, paprika, salt, pepper, bay leaves, remaining broth, and celery leaves. Seal the lid and cook on Meat/Stew for 30 minutes on High. Do a quick release and stir in butter.

Tex-mex Quinoa

Servings:4
Cooking Time: 20 Minutes
Ingredients:
- 1 cup quinoa
- 2 cups water
- 1 cup chunky salsa
- 1 cup corn kernels
- 1 cup canned black beans, drained and rinsed
- 1 teaspoon ground cumin
- ½ teaspoon garlic salt
- ¼ teaspoon ground black pepper

Directions:
1. Add quinoa and water to the Instant Pot. Stir well. Lock lid.
2. Press the Porridge button and cook for the default time of 20 minutes. When timer beeps, quick-release pressure until float valve drops. Unlock lid.
3. Stir in salsa, corn, beans, cumin, garlic salt, and pepper. Let rest in heated pot 5 minutes to warm.
4. Transfer quinoa to a serving dish and fluff with a fork. Serve warm.

Cauliflower & Potato Curry With Cilantro

Servings: 4
Cooking Time: 40 Minutes
Ingredients:
- 1 tbsp vegetable oil
- 10 oz cauliflower florets
- 1 potato, peeled and diced
- 1 tbsp ghee
- 2 tbsp cumin seeds
- 1 onion, minced
- 4 garlic cloves, minced
- 1 tomato, chopped
- 1 jalapeño pepper, minced
- 1 tbsp curry paste
- 1 tbsp ground turmeric
- ½ tsp chili pepper
- Salt and pepper to taste
- 2 tbsp cilantro, chopped

Directions:
1. Warm oil on Sauté. Add in potato and cauliflower and cook for 8 to 10 minutes until lightly browned; season with salt. Set the vegetables in a bowl. Add ghee to the pot. Mix in cumin seeds and cook for 10 seconds until they start to pop; add onion and cook for 3 minutes until softened. Mix in garlic and pepper; cook for 30 seconds.
2. Add in tomato, curry paste, chili pepper, jalapeño pepper, and turmeric; cook for 4 to 6 minutes. Return potato and cauliflower to the pot. Stir in 1 cup water. Seal

the lid and cook on High Pressure for 4 minutes. Quick-release the pressure. Unlock the lid. Top with cilantro and serve.

Sweet Potato Chili

Servings: 4
Cooking Time: 17 Minutes
Ingredients:
- 1 tablespoon olive oil
- 1 small yellow onion, peeled and diced
- 2 medium sweet potatoes, peeled and diced
- 1 can kidney beans, drained and rinsed
- 2 tablespoons chili powder
- 1 tablespoon hot sauce
- 1 teaspoon garlic salt
- 1 can fire-roasted diced tomatoes, including juice
- 2 cups vegetable broth

Directions:
1. Press the Sauté button on the Instant Pot and heat oil. Add onion. Stir-fry 3–5 minutes until onions are translucent.
2. Add remaining ingredients to pot and stir to combine. Press the Cancel button. Lock lid.
3. Press the Manual or Pressure Cook button and adjust time to 12 minutes. When timer beeps, let pressure release naturally until float valve drops. Unlock lid.
4. Ladle chili into bowls. Serve warm.

Savory Spinach With Mashed Potatoes

Servings: 6
Cooking Time: 20 Minutes
Ingredients:
- 3 lb potatoes, peeled
- ½ cup milk
- ⅓ cup butter
- 2 tbsp chopped chives
- Salt and pepper to taste
- 2 cups spinach, chopped

Directions:
1. Cover the potatoes with salted water in your Instant Pot. Seal the lid and cook on High Pressure for 8 minutes. Release the pressure quickly. Drain the potatoes, and reserve the liquid in a bowl. Mash the potatoes. Mix with butter and milk; season with pepper and salt. With reserved cooking liquid, thin the potatoes to attain the desired consistency. Put the spinach in the remaining potato liquid and stir until wilted; Season to taste. Drain and serve with potato mash. Garnish with chives.

Parsley Lentil Soup With Vegetables

Servings: 4
Cooking Time: 20 Minutes
Ingredients:
- 1 tbsp olive oil
- 1 onion, chopped
- 1 cup celery, chopped
- 2 garlic cloves, chopped
- 3 cups vegetable stock
- 1 ½ cups lentils, rinsed
- 4 carrots, halved lengthwise
- ½ tsp salt
- 2 tbsp parsley, chopped

Directions:
1. Warm olive oil on Sauté. Add in onion, garlic, and celery and sauté for 5 minutes until soft. Mix in lentils, carrots, salt, and stock. Seal the lid and cook on High Pressure for 10 minutes. Release the pressure quickly. Serve topped with parsley.

Roman Stewed Beans With Tomatoes

Servings: 6
Cooking Time: 30 Minutes
Ingredients:
- 2 cups cranberry beans
- 2 onions, chopped
- 3 carrots, chopped
- 3 tomatoes, peeled, diced
- 3 tbsp olive oil
- 2 tbsp parsley, chopped
- 2 cups water
- Salt and pepper to taste

Directions:
1. Heat olive oil on Sauté, and stir-fry the onions for 3-4 minutes until translucent. Add in carrots and tomatoes. Stir well and cook for 5 minutes. Stir in beans, salt, black pepper and water, and seal the lid. Cook on High Pressure for 15 minutes. Do a quick release and serve hot sprinkled with fresh parsley.

Quinoa With Brussels Sprouts & Broccoli

Servings: 2
Cooking Time: 25 Minutes
Ingredients:
- 1 cup quinoa, rinsed
- Salt and pepper to taste
- 1 beet, peeled, cubed
- 1 cup broccoli florets
- 1 carrot, chopped
- ½ lb Brussels sprouts
- 2 eggs
- 1 avocado, chopped
- ¼ cup pesto sauce
- Lemon wedges, for serving

Directions:
1. In the pot, mix 2 cups of water, salt, quinoa and pepper. Set trivet over quinoa and set steamer basket on top. To the steamer basket, add eggs, Brussels sprouts, broccoli, beet cubes, carrots, pepper, and salt. Seal the lid and cook for 1 minute on High Pressure. Release pressure naturally for 10 minutes. Remove the steamer basket and trivet from the pot and set the eggs in a bowl of ice water. Peel and halve the eggs. Use a fork to fluff the quinoa. Divide quinoa, broccoli, avocado, carrots, beet, Brussels sprouts, eggs between two bowls, and top with a pesto dollop. Serve with lemon wedges.

Delicious Mushroom Goulash

Servings: 4
Cooking Time: 50 Minutes
Ingredients:
- 6 oz portobello mushrooms, sliced
- 1 cup green peas
- 1 cup pearl onions, minced
- 2 carrots, chopped
- 1 celery stalk, chopped
- 2 garlic cloves, crushed
- 2 potatoes, chopped
- 1 tbsp apple cider vinegar
- 1 tbsp rosemary
- Salt and pepper to taste
- 2 tbsp butter
- 4 cups vegetable stock

Directions:
1. Melt butter on Sauté and stir-fry onions, carrots, celery stalks, and garlic for 2-3 minutes. Season with salt, pepper, and rosemary. Add mushrooms, peas, potatoes, vinegar, and stock and seal the lid. Cook on High Pressure for 30 minutes. When ready, release the pressure naturally.

Quick Cassoulet

Servings: 6
Cooking Time: 45 Minutes
Ingredients:
- 1 tablespoon olive oil
- 1 medium yellow onion, peeled and diced
- 2 cups dried cannellini beans, rinsed and drained
- 2 medium carrots, peeled and diced small
- 1 tablespoon Italian seasoning
- 1 teaspoon garlic salt
- ½ teaspoon ground black pepper
- 2 ½ cups vegetable broth
- 1 can diced tomatoes, including juice
- 4 vegan smoked apple sausages, each cut into 4 sections

Directions:
1. Press the Sauté button on the Instant Pot and heat oil. Add onion and stir-fry 3–5 minutes until onions are translucent. Add beans and toss.
2. Add carrots, Italian seasoning, garlic salt, and pepper.
3. Gently pour in broth and diced tomatoes. Press the Cancel button. Lock lid.
4. Press the Bean button and cook for the default time of 30 minutes. When timer beeps, let pressure release naturally for 10 minutes. Quick-release any additional pressure until float valve drops. Press the Cancel button. Unlock lid. Add sausage.
5. Press the Sauté button on the Instant Pot, press the Adjust button to change the temperature to Less, and simmer bean mixture unlidded 10 minutes to thicken. Transfer to a serving bowl and carefully toss. Serve warm.

Cheddar Cheese Sauce With Broccoli

Servings: 4
Cooking Time: 15 Minutes
Ingredients:
- 1 cup broccoli, chopped
- 1 cup cream cheese
- 1 cup cheddar, shredded

- 3 cups chicken broth
- Salt and pepper to taste
- 2 tsp dried rosemary

Directions:
1. Mix broccoli, cream cheese, cheddar, broth, salt, pepper, and rosemary in a large bowl. Pour the mixture into the Instant Pot. Seal the lid and cook on High Pressure for 8 minutes. Do a quick release. Store for up to 5 days.

Celery & Red Bean Stew

Servings: 4
Cooking Time: 25 Minutes
Ingredients:
- 6 oz red beans, cooked
- 2 carrots, chopped
- 2 celery stalks, chopped
- 1 onion, chopped
- 2 tbsp tomato paste
- 1 bay leaf
- 2 cups vegetable broth
- 3 tbsp olive oil
- 1 tbsp salt
- 2 tbsp parsley, chopped
- 1 tbsp flour

Directions:
1. Warm olive oil on Sauté and stir-fry the onion for 3 minutes. Add celery and carrots. Cook for 5 more minutes. Add red beans, bay leaf, salt, and tomato paste. Stir in 1 tbsp of flour and pour in the vegetable broth. Seal the lid and cook on High Pressure for 5 minutes. Do a natural release for about 10 minutes. Sprinkle with some fresh parsley and serve warm.

Coconut Milk Yogurt With Honey

Servings: 6
Cooking Time: 15 Hours
Ingredients:
- 2 cans coconut milk
- 1 tbsp gelatin
- 1 tbsp honey
- 1 tbsp probiotic powder
- Zest from 1 lime

Directions:
1. Into the pot, stir in gelatin and coconut milk until well dissolved. Seal the lid, Press Yogurt until the display is reading "Boil". Once done, the screen will then display "Yogurt". Ensure milk temperature is at 180°F. Remove steel pot from Pressure cooker base and place into a large ice bath to cool milk for 5 minutes to reach 112°F.
2. Remove the pot from the ice bath and wipe the outside dry. Into the coconut milk mixture, add probiotic powder, honey, and Lime zest, and stir to combine. Return steel pot to the base of the Instant Pot. Seal the lid, press Yogurt, and cook for 10 hours. Once complete, spoon yogurt into glass jars with rings and lids; place in the refrigerator to chill for 4 hours to thicken.

Seasoned Black Beans

Servings: 8
Cooking Time: 45 Minutes
Ingredients:
- 1 cup dried black beans
- 1 tablespoon olive oil
- 1 small onion, peeled and diced
- 3 cloves garlic, minced
- 2 cups vegetable broth
- ¼ teaspoon ground coriander
- ½ teaspoon chili powder
- ¼ teaspoon ground cumin
- ½ teaspoon sea salt
- 2 teaspoons Italian seasoning

Directions:
1. Rinse and drain beans.
2. Press the Sauté button on Instant Pot. Heat olive oil and add onion. Stir-fry 3–5 minutes until onions are translucent. Add garlic and sauté for an additional minute. Deglaze the Instant Pot by adding broth and scraping the bottom and sides of Instant Pot.
3. Add beans and remaining ingredients. Lock lid.
4. Press the Bean button and cook for the default time of 30 minutes. When timer beeps, let pressure release naturally for 10 minutes. Quick-release any additional pressure until float valve drops and then unlock lid.
5. Press Sauté button, press Adjust button to change the temperature to Less, and simmer bean mixture unlidded for 10 minutes to thicken.
6. With a slotted spoon, transfer beans to a serving bowl.

Parmesan Topped Vegetable Mash

Servings: 6
Cooking Time: 15 Minutes
Ingredients:
- 3 lb Yukon gold potatoes, chopped
- 2 cups cauliflower florets
- 1 carrot, chopped
- 1 cup Parmesan, shredded
- ¼ cup butter, melted
- ¼ cup milk
- 1 tsp salt
- 1 garlic clove, minced
- 2 tbsp parsley, chopped

Directions:
1. Into the pot, add potatoes, cauliflower, carrot and salt; cover with enough water. Seal the lid and cook on High Pressure for 10 minutes. Release the pressure quickly. Drain the vegetables and mash them with a potato masher. Add garlic, butter, and milk. Whisk until well incorporated. Top with Parmesan cheese and parsley.

Cauliflower Charcuterie

Servings: 4
Cooking Time: 2 Minutes
Ingredients:
- ¼ cup hot sauce
- ¼ cup teriyaki sauce
- 1 cup water
- 1 large head cauliflower, chopped into bite-sized florets
- ½ cup ranch dip
- ½ cup blue cheese dip
- 4 medium stalks celery, cut into 1" sections

Directions:
1. Add hot sauce to a medium bowl. Add teriyaki sauce to another medium bowl. Set aside.
2. Add water to the Instant Pot. Add steamer basket to pot and add cauliflower in basket in an even layer. Lock lid.
3. Press the Manual or Pressure Cook button and adjust time to 2 minutes. When timer beeps, quick-release pressure until float valve drops. Unlock lid.
4. Transfer half of cauliflower to bowl with hot sauce and toss. Transfer other half of cauliflower to bowl with teriyaki sauce and toss. Serve warm with dipping sauces and celery.

Mushroom & Ricotta Cheese Manicotti

Servings: 4
Cooking Time: 35 Minutes
Ingredients:
- 6 oz button mushrooms, chopped
- 8 oz pack manicotti pasta
- 12 oz spinach, torn
- 3 oz ricotta cheese
- ¼ cup milk
- 3 oz butter
- ¼ tbsp salt
- 1 tbsp sour cream

Directions:
1. Melt butter on Sauté and add mushrooms. Cook until soft, 5 minutes. Add spinach and milk and continue to cook for 6 minutes. Stir in cheese and season with salt. Line a baking dish with parchment paper. Fill manicotti with spinach mixture. Transfer them on the baking sheet. Pour 1 cup water into the Instant Pot and insert a trivet. Lay the baking sheet on the trivet. Seal the lid and cook on High Pressure for 15 minutes. Do a quick release. Top with sour cream and serve.

Homemade Gazpacho Soup

Servings: 4
Cooking Time: 2 Hours 20 Minutes
Ingredients:
- 1 lb trimmed carrots
- 1 lb tomatoes, chopped
- 1 cucumber, peeled, cubed
- ¼ cup olive oil
- 2 tbsp lemon juice
- 1 red onion, chopped
- 2 cloves garlic
- 2 tbsp white wine vinegar
- Salt and pepper to taste

Directions:
1. Add carrots, salt, and enough water to cover the carrots. Seal the lid and cook for 10 minutes on High Pressure. Do a quick release. In a blender, add carrots, cucumber, red onion, pepper, garlic, oil, tomatoes, lemon juice, vinegar, 4 cups of water, and salt. Blend until very smooth. Place gazpacho into a serving bowl, chill while covered for 2 hours. Serve and enjoy!

Carrot & Chickpea Boil With Tomatoes

Servings: 4
Cooking Time: 25 Minutes

Ingredients:
- ½ cup button mushrooms, chopped
- 1 cup canned chickpeas
- 1 onion, peeled, chopped
- 1 lb string beans, trimmed
- 1 apple, cubed
- ½ cup raisins
- 2 carrots, chopped
- 2 garlic cloves, crushed
- 4 cherry tomatoes
- 1 tbsp grated ginger
- ½ cup orange juice

Directions:

1. Place mushrooms, chickpeas, onion, beans, apple, raisins, carrots, garlic, cherry tomatoes, ginger, and orange juice in the Instant Pot. Pour enough water to cover. Cook on High Pressure for 8 minutes. Do a natural release for 10 minutes. Serve warm.

Fish & Seafood

Paprika Salmon With Dill Sauce

Servings: 2
Cooking Time: 15 Minutes
Ingredients:
- 2 salmon fillets
- ¼ tsp paprika
- Salt and pepper to taste
- ¼ cup fresh dill
- Juice from ½ lemon
- Sea salt to taste
- ¼ cup olive oil

Directions:
1. In a food processor, blend the olive oil, lemon juice, dill, and seas salt until creamy; reserve. To the cooker, add 1 cup water and place a steamer basket. Arrange salmon fillets skin-side down on the steamer basket. Sprinkle the salmon with paprika, salt, and pepper. Seal the lid and cook for 3 minutes on High Pressure. Release the pressure quickly. Top the fillets with dill sauce to serve.

Mediterranean Cod With Capers

Servings: 4
Cooking Time: 15 Minutes
Ingredients:
- 4 cod fillets, boneless
- ½ cup white wine
- 1 tsp oregano
- Salt and pepper to taste
- ¼ cup capers

Directions:
1. Pour the white wine and ½ cup of water in your Instant Pot and fit in a trivet. Place cod fillets on the trivet.
2. Sprinkle with oregano, salt, and pepper. Seal the lid, select Steam, and cook for 3 minutes on Low. Once ready, perform a quick pressure release. Top the cod with capers and drizzle with the sauce to serve.

Easy Seafood Paella

Servings: 4
Cooking Time: 20 Minutes
Ingredients:
- 1 cup tiger prawns, peeled and deveined
- 1 lb mussels, cleaned and debearded
- ½ tsp guindilla (cayenne pepper)
- ½ lb clams
- 2 tbsp olive oil
- 1 onion, chopped
- 2 garlic cloves, minced
- 1 red bell pepper, chopped
- 1 cup rice
- 2 cups clam juice
- ¾ cup green peas, frozen
- 1 tbsp parsley, chopped
- 1 tbsp turmeric
- 1 whole lemon, quartered

Directions:
1. Warm the olive oil in your Instant Pot on Sauté. Add in prawns, red pepper, onion, and garlic and cook for 3 minutes. Stir in rice for 1 minute and pour in clam juice, turmeric, mussels, and clams. Seal the lid, select Manual, and cook for 5 minutes on High pressure. When ready, perform a quick pressure release and unlock the lid. Stir in green peas and guindilla for 3-4 minutes. Top with lemon quarters and parsley. Serve immediately.

Herby Crab Legs With Lemon

Servings: 4
Cooking Time: 10 Minutes
Ingredients:
- 3 lb king crab legs, broken in half
- 1 tsp rosemary
- 1 tsp thyme
- 1 tsp dill
- ¼ cup butter, melted
- Salt and pepper to taste
- 1 lemon, cut into wedges

Directions:
1. Pour 1 cup of water into your Instant Pot and fit in a trivet. Season the crab legs with rosemary, thyme, dill, salt, and pepper; place on the trivet. Seal the lid, select Manual, and cook for 3 minutes. When ready, perform a quick pressure release. Remove crab legs to a bowl and drizzle with melted butter. Serve with lemon wedges.

Chinese Shrimp With Green Beans

Servings: 2
Cooking Time: 20 Minutes
Ingredients:
- 1 tbsp sesame oil
- 1 lb shrimp, deveined
- ½ cup diced onion
- 2 cloves garlic, minced
- 1 carrot, cut into strips
- ½ lb green beans, chopped
- 2 cups vegetable stock
- 3 tbsp soy sauce
- 2 tbsp rice wine vinegar
- 10 oz lo mein egg noodles
- ½ tsp toasted sesame seeds
- Sea Salt and pepper to taste

Directions:
1. Warm oil on Sauté. Stir-fry the shrimp for 5 minutes; set aside. Add in garlic and onion and cook for 3 minutes until fragrant. Mix in soy sauce, carrot, stock, beans, and rice wine vinegar. Add in noodles and ensure they are covered. Season with pepper and salt. Seal the lid and cook on High Pressure for 5 minutes. Release the pressure quickly. Place the main in 2 plates. Add the reserved shrimp, sprinkle with sesame seeds, and serve.

Galician-style Octopus

Servings: 6
Cooking Time: 30 Minutes
Ingredients:
- 1 lb potatoes, sliced into rounds
- 2 lb whole octopus, cleaned and sliced
- 1 tbsp Spanish paprika
- 3 tbsp olive oil
- Salt and pepper to taste

Directions:
1. Place the potatoes in your Instant Pot and cover them with water. Place a trivet over the potatoes. Season the octopus with salt and pepper and place it onto the trivet. Seal the lid, select Manual, and cook for 15 minutes.
2. Once done, perform a quick pressure release and unlock the lid. Remove the octopus and let cool, then slice it into slices about half-inch thick. Transfer the sliced potatoes to a baking sheet and arrange octopus slices over the potatoes. Drizzle with olive oil and place under the broiler for 5 minutes. Sprinkle with paprika and serve.

Basil Clams With Garlic & White Wine

Servings: 4
Cooking Time: 15 Minutes
Ingredients:
- 1 lb clams, scrubbed
- 2 tbsp butter
- 4 green garlic, chopped
- 1 tbsp lemon juice
- ½ cup white wine
- ½ cup chicken stock
- Salt and pepper to taste
- 2 tbsp basil, chopped

Directions:
1. Melt the butter in your Instant Pot on Sauté. Add in the garlic and clams and cook for 3-4 minutes. Stir in lemon juice and chicken stock, white wine, salt, and pepper and seal the lid. Select Manual and cook for 3 minutes on High pressure. Once done, perform a quick pressure release and unlock the lid. Discard unopened clams. Serve topped with basil.

Buttery Cod With Scallions

Servings: 4
Cooking Time: 15 Minutes
Ingredients:
- 4 cod fillets
- 1 fennel bulb, sliced
- Salt and pepper to taste
- 2 tbsp scallions, chopped
- 1 lemon, cut into wedges
- 1 tbsp garlic powder
- 2 tbsp butter, melted

Directions:
1. Pour 1 cup of water into your Instant Pot; fit in a trivet. Brush the cod fillets with butter and season with garlic, salt, and pepper. Place them on the trivet and top with fennel slices. Seal the lid, Select Manual, and cook for 5 minutes on High. Once ready, perform a quick pressure release. Sprinkle with scallions and serve with lemon wedges.

Steamed Halibut Packets

Servings: 4
Cooking Time: 20 Minutes
Ingredients:
- 4 halibut fillets
- 1 lb cherry tomatoes, halved
- 1 cup olives, chopped
- 2 tbsp olive oil
- 1 garlic clove, minced
- ½ tsp thyme
- Salt and pepper to taste
- Arugula for garnish

Directions:
1. Pour 1 cup of water into your Instant Pot and insert a trivet. Divide the halibut fillets, cherry tomatoes, and olives between 4 sheets of aluminum foil. Drizzle with olive oil and season with salt, pepper, garlic, and thyme. Close the packets and seal the edges. Place them on the trivet. Secure the lid, select Steam, and cook for 4 minutes on Low. When done, allow a natural release for 10 minutes. Serve scattered with arugula.

Party Shrimp With & Rice Veggies

Servings: 4
Cooking Time: 36 Minutes
Ingredients:
- ¼ cup olive oil
- 1 onion, chopped
- 1 red bell pepper, diced
- 2 garlic cloves, minced
- 1 tsp turmeric
- Salt and pepper to taste
- 1 cup rice
- ¼ cup green peas
- 2 cups fish broth
- 1 lb shrimp, deveined
- Chopped fresh parsley
- 1 lemon, cut into wedges

Directions:
1. Warm oil on Sauté. Add in bell pepper and onion and garlic and cook for 5 minutes until fragrant. Season with pepper, salt, and turmeric and cook for 1 minute. Stir in fish broth and rice. Seal the lid and cook on High Pressure for 15 minutes. Release the pressure quickly. Stir in green peas and shrimp and cook for 5 minutes on Sauté. Serve with parsley and lemon.

Cilantro Cod On Millet With Peppers

Servings: 4
Cooking Time: 15 Minutes
Ingredients:
- 2 tbsp olive oil
- 1 cup millet
- 1 yellow bell pepper, diced
- 1 red bell pepper, diced
- 2 cups chicken broth
- 1 cup breadcrumbs
- 4 tbsp melted butter
- ¼ cup minced fresh cilantro
- 4 cod fillets
- 1 lemon, zested and juiced

Directions:
1. Combine oil, millet, yellow and red bell peppers in the pot, and cook for 1 minute on Sauté. Mix in the chicken broth. Place a trivet on to. In a bowl, mix crumbs, butter, cilantro, lemon zest, and juice. Spoon the bread crumb mixture evenly on the cod fillet. Lay the fish on the trivet. Seal the lid and cook on High for 6 minutes. Do a quick release and serve immediately.

Tilapia Fillets With Hazelnut Crust

Servings: 4
Cooking Time: 15 Minutes
Ingredients:
- 4 tilapia fillets
- 2 tsp olive oil
- ¼ tsp lemon pepper
- 2 tbsp Dijon mustard
- ½ cup chopped hazelnuts
- 2 tbsp parsley, chopped
- Salt and pepper to taste

Directions:
1. Pour 1 cup of water into your Instant Pot and fit in a trivet. Mix the olive oil, lemon pepper, and Dijon mustard in a bowl. Rub each fillet with mustard mixture, then roll them in the hazelnuts to coat.
2. Place the fillets on the trivet, sprinkle with salt and pepper, and seal the lid. Select Manual, and cook for 5

minutes on High. When done, perform a quick pressure release. Unlock the lid. Serve scattered with parsley.

Herbed Poached Salmon

Servings: 2
Cooking Time: 20 Minutes
Ingredients:
- 2 salmon fillets, skin-on
- 1 cup chicken broth
- ¼ cup dry white wine
- 1 tsp lemon zest
- ¼ tsp basil
- ¼ tsp oregano
- ¼ tsp thyme
- ¼ tsp marjoram
- 1 tbsp garlic oil
- 4 scallions, chopped
- Salt and pepper to taste

Directions:
1. Pour chicken broth and white wine in your Instant Pot and fit in a trivet. In a bowl, combine basil, oregano, thyme, marjoram, lemon zest, garlic oil, salt, and pepper. Spread the rub evenly onto the salmon and place it on the trivet. Seal the lid, select Manual, and cook for 5 minutes on High pressure. Once over, allow a natural release for 5 minutes, perform a quick pressure release, and unlock the lid. Sprinkle with scallions and serve.

Littleneck Clams In Garlic Wine Broth

Servings: 4
Cooking Time: 8 Minutes
Ingredients:
- 2 pounds fresh littleneck clams, cleaned and debearded
- 2 tablespoons olive oil
- 1 medium yellow onion, peeled and diced
- 4 cloves garlic, peeled and minced
- ½ cup dry white wine
- ½ cup vegetable broth
- ½ teaspoon salt
- 4 tablespoons chopped fresh parsley

Directions:
1. Let clams soak in water 30 minutes. Rinse several times. This will help purge any sand trapped in the shells.

2. Press the Sauté button on the Instant Pot and heat oil. Add onion and sauté 3–5 minutes until translucent. Add garlic and cook an additional 1 minute. Stir in wine, broth, and salt and let cook 2 minutes. Press the Cancel button.
3. Insert steamer basket. Place clams in basket. Lock lid.
4. Press the Manual or Pressure Cook button and adjust time to 0 minutes. When timer beeps, quick-release pressure until float valve drops. Unlock lid.
5. Remove clams and discard any that haven't opened. Transfer clams to four bowls and pour liquid from the Instant Pot equally among bowls. Garnish each bowl with 1 tablespoon parsley. Serve immediately.

Steamed Shrimp And Asparagus

Servings: 2
Cooking Time: 1 Minute
Ingredients:
- 1 cup water
- 1 bunch asparagus
- 1 teaspoon sea salt, divided
- 1 pound shrimp, peeled and deveined
- ½ lemon
- 2 tablespoons butter, cut into 2 pats

Directions:
1. Pour water into Instant Pot. Insert trivet. Place steamer basket onto trivet.
2. Prepare asparagus by finding the natural snap point on the stalks and discarding the woody ends.
3. Spread the asparagus on the bottom of the steamer basket. Sprinkle with ½ teaspoon salt. Add the shrimp. Squeeze lemon into the Instant Pot, then sprinkle shrimp with remaining ½ teaspoon salt. Place pats of butter on shrimp. Lock lid.
4. Press the Manual button and adjust time to 1 minute. When the timer beeps, quick-release the pressure until the float valve drops and then unlock lid.
5. Transfer shrimp and asparagus to a platter and serve.

Stuffed Tench With Herbs & Lemon

Servings: 2
Cooking Time: 20 Minutes
Ingredients:
- 1 tench, cleaned, gutted
- 1 lemon, quartered
- 2 tbsp olive oil
- 1 tsp rosemary, chopped
- ¼ tsp dried thyme

- 2 garlic cloves, crushed

Directions:

1. In a bowl, mix olive oil, garlic, rosemary, and thyme. Stir to combine. Brush the fish with the previously prepared mixture and stuff with lemon. Pour 4 cups of water into the Instant Pot, set the steamer tray, and place the fish on top. Seal the lid and cook on Steam for 15 minutes on High Pressure. Do a quick release. Unlock the lid. For a crispier taste, briefly brown the fish in a grill pan.

Low-country Boil

Servings: 6
Cooking Time: 5 Minutes
Ingredients:

- 1 large sweet onion, peeled and chopped
- 4 cloves garlic, quartered
- 6 small red potatoes, cut in sixths
- 3 ears corn, cut in thirds
- 1½ pounds fully cooked andouille sausage, cut in 1" sections
- 1 pound frozen tail-on shrimp
- 1 tablespoon Old Bay Seasoning
- 2 cups chicken broth
- 1 lemon, cut into 6 wedges
- ½ cup chopped fresh parsley

Directions:

1. Layer onions in an even layer in the Instant Pot. Scatter the garlic on top of onions. Add red potatoes in an even layer, then do the same for the corn and sausage. Add the shrimp and sprinkle with Old Bay Seasoning. Pour in broth.
2. Squeeze lemon wedges into the Instant Pot and place squeezed lemon wedges into the Instant Pot. Lock lid.
3. Press the Manual button and adjust time to 5 minutes. When timer beeps, quick-release the pressure until float valve drops and then unlock lid. Transfer ingredients to a serving platter and garnish with parsley.

Herby Trout With Farro & Green Beans

Servings: 4
Cooking Time: 20 Minutes
Ingredients:

- 1 cup farro
- 2 cups water
- 4 skinless trout fillets
- 8 oz green beans
- 1 tbsp olive oil
- Salt and pepper to taste
- 4 tbsp melted butter
- ½ tbsp sugar
- ½ tbsp lemon juice
- ½ tsp dried rosemary
- 2 garlic cloves, minced
- ½ tsp dried thyme

Directions:

1. Pour the farro and water into the pot and mix with green beans and olive oil. Season with salt and black pepper. In another bowl, mix the remaining black pepper and salt, butter, sugar, lemon juice, rosemary, garlic, and thyme.
2. Coat the trout with the buttery herb sauce. Insert a trivet in the pot and lay the trout fillets on the trivet. Seal the lid and cook on High Pressure for 12 minutes. Do a quick release and serve immediately.

Savory Cod Fillets In Maple-lemon Sauce

Servings: 4
Cooking Time: 15 Minutes
Ingredients:

- 1 lb cod fillets, skinless and boneless
- 1 cup maple syrup
- ½ cup soy sauce
- 3 garlic cloves, chopped
- 1 lemon, juiced
- 1 tbsp butter

Directions:

1. In a bowl, mix maple syrup, soy sauce, garlic, and lemon juice. Stir until combined and set aside. Grease the pot with butter. Place the fillets at the bottom and pour over the maple mixture. Seal the lid and cook on Steam for 8 minutes on High. Release the pressure naturally. Serve.

Quick Shrimp Gumbo With Sausage

Servings: 4
Cooking Time: 30 Minutes
Ingredients:
- 1 lb jumbo shrimp
- 2 tbsp olive oil
- 1/3 cup flour
- 1 ½ tsp Cajun seasoning
- 1 onion, chopped
- 1 red bell pepper, chopped
- 2 celery stalks, chopped
- 2 garlic cloves, minced
- 1 serrano pepper, minced
- 2 ½ cups chicken broth
- 6 oz andouille sausage, sliced
- 2 green onions, finely sliced
- Salt and pepper to taste

Directions:
1. Heat olive oil on Sauté. Whisk in the flour with a wooden spoon and cook 3 minutes, stirring constantly. Stir in Cajun seasoning, onion, bell pepper, celery, garlic, and serrano pepper for about 5 minutes. Pour in the chicken broth, ¾ cup water, and andouille sausage. Seal and cook for 6 minutes on High Pressure. Do a natural pressure for 5 minutes. Stir the shrimp into the gumbo to eat it up for 3 minutes. Adjust the seasoning. Ladle the gumbo into bowls and garnish with the green onions.

Jalapeño Shrimp With Herbs & Lemon

Servings: 4
Cooking Time: 25 Minutes
Ingredients:
- 1 lb shrimp, deveined
- ½ cup olive oil
- 1 tsp garlic powder
- 1 tsp rosemary, chopped
- 1 tsp thyme, chopped
- ½ tsp basil, chopped
- ½ tsp sage, chopped
- ½ tsp salt
- 1 tsp jalapeño pepper

Directions:
1. Pour 1 cup of water into the inner pot. In a bowl, mix oil, garlic, rosemary, thyme, basil, sage, salt, and jalapeño pepper. Brush the marinade over the shrimp. Insert a steamer rack in the pot and arrange the shrimp on top.
2. Seal the lid and cook on Steam for 3 minutes on High. Release the steam naturally for 10 minutes. Press Sauté and stir-fry for 2 more minutes or until golden brown.

Cheesy Shrimp Scampi

Servings: 4
Cooking Time: 10 Minutes
Ingredients:
- 1 lb shrimp, deveined
- 2 tbsp olive oil
- 1 clove garlic, minced
- 1 tbsp tomato paste
- 10 oz canned tomatoes, diced
- ½ cup dry white wine
- 1 tsp red chili pepper
- 1 tbsp parsley, chopped
- Salt and pepper to taste
- 1 cup Grana Padano, grated

Directions:
1. Warm the olive oil in your Instant Pot on Sauté. Add in garlic and cook for 1 minute. Stir in shrimp, tomato paste, tomatoes, white wine, chili pepper, parsley, salt, pepper, and ¼ cup of water and seal the lid. Select Manual and cook for 3 minutes on High pressure. Once done, perform a quick pressure release and unlock the lid. Serve garnished with Grana Padano cheese.

Seafood Pilaf

Servings: 6
Cooking Time: 35 Minutes
Ingredients:
- 1 lb chopped catfish fillets
- 2 cups mussels and shrimp
- 4 tbsp olive oil
- 1 onion, diced
- 2 garlic cloves, minced
- ½ tsp cayenne pepper
- ½ tsp basil
- ½ tsp oregano
- 1 red bell pepper, diced
- 1 green bell pepper, diced
- 2 cups Jasmine rice
- A few saffron threads
- 3 cups fish stock

- Salt and pepper to taste

Directions:

1. Warm the olive oil in your Instant Pot on Sauté. Add in onion, garlic, and bell peppers and cook for 4 minutes. Add in catfish, rice, and saffron and cook for another 2 minutes. Add mussels, shrimps, cayenne pepper, basil, oregano, stock, salt, and pepper, stir, and seal the lid. Select Manual and cook for 6 minutes. When done, allow a natural release for 10 minutes. Serve.

Creole Seafood Gumbo

Servings: 4
Cooking Time: 20 Minutes
Ingredients:

- 12 oz pollock filets, cut into chunks
- 1 lb medium raw shrimp, deveined
- Salt and pepper to taste
- 1 tbsp creole seasoning
- 1 olive oil
- 1 yellow onion, diced
- 2 celery ribs, diced
- 1 cup chicken broth
- 14 oz diced tomatoes
- ¼ cup tomato paste
- 2 bay leaves
- 6 oz okra, trimmed

Directions:

1. Sprinkle the pollock with salt, pepper, and creole seasoning. Warm the olive oil in your Instant Pot on Sauté. Add in the fish and cook for 4 minutes. Set aside. Add onions and celery to the pot and cook for 2 minutes.

2. Put in chicken broth, tomatoes, tomato paste, bay leaves, okra, shrimp, and cooked fish and seal the lid. Select Manual and cook for 5 minutes on High pressure. When ready, perform a quick pressure release. Serve.

Mussels With Lemon & White Wine

Servings: 5
Cooking Time: 10 Minutes
Ingredients:

- 2 lb mussels, cleaned and debearded
- 1 cup white wine
- ½ cup water
- 1 tsp garlic powder
- Juice from 1 lemon

Directions:

1. In the pot, mix garlic powder, water, and wine. Put the mussels into the steamer basket; rounded-side should be placed facing upwards to fit as many as possible.

2. Insert a rack into the cooker and lower the steamer basket onto the rack. Seal the lid and cook on Low Pressure for 1 minute. Release the pressure quickly. Remove unopened mussels. Coat the mussels with the wine mixture and lemon juice and serve.

Red Onion Trout Fillets With Olives

Servings: 6
Cooking Time: 15 Minutes+ Marinating Time
Ingredients:

- 2 lb trout fillets, skin on
- ½ cup olive oil
- ¼ cup apple cider vinegar
- 1 red onion, chopped
- 1 lemon, sliced
- 2 garlic cloves, crushed
- 1 tbsp rosemary, chopped
- Salt and pepper to taste
- 3 cups fish stock
- 12 black olives

Directions:

1. In a bowl, mix oil, apple cider, onion, garlic, rosemary, sea salt, and pepper. Submerge the fillets into this mixture and refrigerate for 1 hour. Pour 4 tbsp of the marinade into your Instant Pot and add in the stock. Add the fish, seal the lid, and cook on High pressure for 4 minutes. Do a quick release. Serve with lemon and olives.

Orange Roughy With Zucchini

Servings:2
Cooking Time: 3 Minutes
Ingredients:

- 1 cup water
- 1 large zucchini, thinly sliced
- 2 orange roughy fillets, cubed
- Juice of 1 medium lemon
- 1 teaspoon salt
- ½ teaspoon ground black pepper
- 4 tablespoons unsalted butter, cut into 8 pats
- 2 tablespoons chopped fresh parsley

Directions:

1. Add water to the Instant Pot and insert steamer basket.

2. Add zucchini to basket in an even layer. Add orange roughy fillets on top. Squeeze lemon juice over fish. Season with salt and pepper. Distribute butter pats on fish and zucchini. Lock lid.

3. Press the Manual or Pressure Cook button and adjust time to 3 minutes. When timer beeps, quick-release pressure until float valve drops. Unlock lid.

4. Transfer fish and zucchini to two plates. Garnish with parsley. Serve warm.

Creamed Crab

Servings:4
Cooking Time: 8 Minutes
Ingredients:
- 4 tablespoons butter
- ½ stalk celery, finely diced
- 1 small red onion, peeled and finely diced
- 1 pound uncooked lump crabmeat
- ¼ cup chicken broth
- ½ cup heavy cream
- ½ teaspoon sea salt
- ½ teaspoon ground black pepper

Directions:
1. Press the Sauté button on Instant Pot. Add the butter and melt. Add the celery and red onion. Stir-fry for 3–5 minutes until celery begins to soften. Stir in the crabmeat and broth. Lock lid.

2. Press the Manual button and adjust time to 3 minutes. Press the Pressure button to change the pressure to Less. When timer beeps, quick-release pressure until float valve drops and then unlock lid.

3. Carefully stir in the cream, add salt and pepper, and serve warm.

Trout In Herb Sauce

Servings:4
Cooking Time: 5 Minutes
Ingredients:
- Trout
- 4 (½-pound) fresh river trout
- 1 teaspoon sea salt
- 4 cups torn lettuce leaves, divided
- 1 teaspoon white wine vinegar
- ½ cup water
- Herb Sauce
- ½ cup minced fresh flat-leaf parsley
- 2 teaspoons Italian seasoning
- 1 small shallot, peeled and minced
- 2 tablespoons mayonnaise
- ½ teaspoon fresh lemon juice
- ¼ teaspoon sugar
- Pinch of salt
- 2 tablespoons sliced almonds, toasted

Directions:
1. For Trout: Rinse the trout inside and out; pat dry. Sprinkle with salt inside and out. Put 3 cups lettuce leaves in the bottom of the Instant Pot. Arrange the trout over the top of the lettuce and top fish with the remaining lettuce.

2. Pour vinegar and water into pot. Lock lid.

3. Press the Manual button and adjust time to 3 minutes. When the timer beeps, let pressure release naturally for 3 minutes. Quick-release any additional pressure until float valve drops and then unlock lid.

4. Transfer fish to a serving plate. Peel and discard the skin from the fish. Remove and discard the heads if desired.

5. For Herb Sauce: In a small bowl, mix together the parsley, Italian seasoning, shallot, mayonnaise, lemon juice, sugar, and salt. Evenly divide among the fish, spreading it over them. Sprinkle toasted almonds over the top of the sauce. Serve.

Chili Squid

Servings: 4
Cooking Time: 35 Minutes
Ingredients:
- 1 lb squid, sliced into rings
- 1 tsp onion powder
- 2 tbsp flour
- 1 garlic clove, minced
- 1 tbsp chives
- ¼ tsp chili pepper, chopped
- ¼ tsp smoked paprika
- 1 tbsp lemon juice
- 1 cup vegetable broth
- 2 tbsp butter
- Salt and pepper to taste
- 2 tbsp parsley, chopped

Directions:

1. Mix the onion powder, smoked paprika, flour, garlic, chives, chili pepper, salt, and pepper in a bowl. Add in the squid slices and toss to coat. Let sit for 10 minutes.

2. Melt the butter in your Instant Pot on Sauté. Place in the squid mixture and cook for 3-4 minutes. Pour in the vegetable broth and seal the lid. Cook on Manual for 12 minutes on High. Once done, perform a quick pressure release and unlock the lid. Serve sprinkled with parsley.

Red Wine Squid

Servings: 4
Cooking Time: 25 Minutes
Ingredients:
- 2 lb squid, chopped
- 2 tbsp olive oil
- Salt and pepper to taste
- ½ cup red wine
- ½ fennel bulb, sliced
- 28 oz can crushed tomatoes
- 1 red onion, sliced
- 2 garlic cloves, minced
- 1 tsp Italian seasoning
- ½ cup parsley, chopped

Directions:
1. Mix the olive oil, squid, salt, and pepper in a bowl. Pour the red wine, tomatoes, onion, garlic, Italian seasoning, and fennel in your Instant Pot and fit in a steamer basket. Put in the squid and seal the lid. Select Manual and cook for 4 minutes on High pressure. When ready, allow a natural release for 10 minutes, then perform a quick pressure release. Serve scattered with parsley.

Poultry

Chicken Wings In Yogurt-garlic Sauce

Servings: 6
Cooking Time: 35 Minutes
Ingredients:
- 12 chicken wings
- 3 tbsp olive oil
- Salt to taste
- 3 cups chicken broth
- ½ cup sour cream
- 1 cup yogurt
- 2 garlic cloves, minced

Directions:
1. Heat oil on Sauté in your Instant Pot. Brown the wings for 6 minutes, turning once. Pour in broth, salt, and seal the lid. Cook on Poultry for 15 minutes on High. Do a natural release. Unlock the lid. In a bowl, mix sour cream, yogurt, salt, and garlic. Drizzle with yogurt sauce. Serve.

Chicken Taco Salad Bowls

Servings: 4
Cooking Time: 4 Minutes
Ingredients:
- 2 teaspoons olive oil
- 1 pound ground chicken
- 1 packet taco seasoning mix
- ⅛ teaspoon hot sauce
- ½ cup water
- 4 cups shredded iceberg lettuce
- ¼ cup shredded Mexican-blend cheese
- 1 cup crushed tortilla chips

Directions:
1. Press the Sauté button on the Instant Pot. Heat olive oil. Add chicken and brown 3 minutes.
2. Stir in taco seasoning mix, hot sauce, and water. Press the Cancel button. Lock lid.
3. Press the Manual or Pressure Cook button and adjust time to 1 minute. When timer beeps, quick-release pressure until float valve drops. Unlock lid. Stir mixture.
4. Line four bowls with lettuce. Using a slotted spoon, transfer chicken mixture to bowls. Garnish with cheese and tortilla chips. Serve warm.

Hungarian-style Turkey Stew

Servings: 4
Cooking Time: 40 Minutes
Ingredients:
- 1 lb chopped turkey pieces
- 2 tbsp butter
- 1 tsp paprika
- 1 can diced tomatoes
- 1 red onion, sliced
- 2 garlic cloves, chopped
- 1 red bell pepper, chopped
- 1 green bell pepper, chopped
- 1 cup chicken stock
- Salt and pepper to taste
- 6 tbsp sour cream
- 2 tbsp parsley, chopped

Directions:
1. Melt butter in your Instant Pot on Sauté and cook the turkey for 5 minutes, stirring occasionally. Add in onion, garlic, and bell peppers and sauté for another 3 minutes. Stir in paprika, tomatoes, and stock and seal the lid. Select Manual and cook for 20 minutes on High pressure. Once over, perform a quick pressure release and unlock the lid. Adjust the seasoning. Top with sour cream and parsley.

Honey-lemon Chicken With Vegetables

Servings: 4
Cooking Time: 35 Minutes
Ingredients:
- 4 skin-on, bone-in chicken legs
- 2 tbsp olive oil
- Salt and pepper to taste
- 4 cloves garlic, minced
- 1 tsp fresh chopped thyme
- ½ cup dry white wine
- 1 ¼ cups chicken stock

- 1 cup carrots, chopped
- 1 cup parsnips, chopped
- 3 tomatoes, chopped
- 1 tbsp honey
- 4 lemon slices

Directions:

1. Season the chicken with pepper and salt. Warm oil on Sauté in your Instant Pot. Cook the chicken legs for 6-8 minutes on all sides until browned; reserve. Sauté thyme and garlic in the chicken fat for 1 minute until soft and lightly golden. Add in wine to deglaze, scrape the pot's bottom to get rid of any brown bits of food. Simmer for 2-3 minutes until slightly reduced in volume.

2. Add stock, carrots, parsnip, tomatoes, pepper, and salt into the pot. Lay steam rack over veggies. Put the chicken legs on the rack. Drizzle with honey, then top with lemon slices. Seal the lid and cook on High Pressure for 12 minutes. Release pressure quickly. On a large platter, arrange the chicken legs and drained veggies. Sprinkle with thyme and serve.

Turkey Cakes With Ginger Gravy

Servings: 4
Cooking Time: 25 Minutes
Ingredients:

- 1 lb ground turkey
- ¼ cup breadcrumbs
- ¼ cup grated Parmesan
- ½ tsp garlic powder
- 2 green onions, chopped
- Salt and pepper to taste
- 2 tbsp olive oil
- 2 cups tomatoes, diced
- ¼ cup chicken broth
- Ginger sauce
- 4 tbsp soy sauce
- 2 tbsp canola oil
- 2 tbsp rice vinegar
- 1 garlic clove, minced
- 1 tsp ginger, grated
- ½ tbsp honey
- ¼ tsp black pepper
- ½ tbsp cornstarch

Directions:

1. Combine turkey, breadcrumbs, green onions, garlic powder, salt, pepper, and Parmesan cheese in a bowl. Mix with your hands and shape meatballs out of the mixture. In another bowl, mix soy sauce, canola oil, rice vinegar, garlic clove, ginger, honey, pepper, and cornstarch. Warm the olive oil in your Instant Pot on Sauté.

2. Place in meatballs and cook for 4 minutes on all sides. Pour in ginger gravy, tomatoes, and chicken stock and seal the lid. Select Manual and cook for 10 minutes on High pressure. Once over, perform a quick pressure release and unlock the lid. Serve in individual bowls.

Turkey Sausage With Brussels Sprouts

Servings: 4
Cooking Time: 40 Minutes
Ingredients:

- 1 lb turkey sausage, sliced
- 2 tbsp olive oil
- 1 yellow onion, chopped
- 2 garlic cloves, minced
- ½ lb Brussels sprouts, sliced
- ¼ cup chicken broth
- 1 tsp yellow mustard
- 1 tsp balsamic vinegar
- Salt and pepper to taste

Directions:

1. Warm the olive oil in your Instant Pot on Sauté. Place in onion and garlic and cook for 2 minutes. Add in turkey sausage and cook for 5 more minutes. Stir in Brussels sprouts, mustard, vinegar, salt, and pepper for 3 minutes. Pour in chicken broth. Seal the lid, select Manual, and cook for 15 minutes on High pressure. When ready, allow a natural release for 5 minutes, then a quick pressure release, and unlock the lid. Serve right away.

Dijon Mustard Chicken Breast

Servings: 2
Cooking Time: 40 Minutes
Ingredients:

- 1 lb chicken
- ¼ cup apple cider vinegar
- 2 tbsp Dijon mustard
- Salt and pepper to taste
- 2 tbsp olive oil
- 2 cups chicken stock

Directions:

1. Season the chicken with salt and black pepper. Place in your Instant Pot and pour in the stock. Seal the lid and cook on Manual for 20 minutes. Do a quick release and remove the meat along with the stock.

2. In a bowl, mix olive oil, mustard, and vinegar. Pour into the pot and press Sauté. Place the chicken in this mixture and cook for 10 minutes, turning once. When done, remove from the pot and drizzle with the sauce.

Pumpkin & Wild Rice Cajun Chicken

Servings: 6
Cooking Time: 30 Minutes
Ingredients:

- 6 chicken thighs, skinless
- Salt and pepper to taste
- ½ tsp ground red pepper
- ½ tsp onion powder
- 1 tsp Cajun seasoning
- 1/8 tsp smoked paprika
- 2 tbsp olive oil
- 1 cup pumpkin, cubed
- 2 celery stalks, diced
- 2 onions, diced
- 3 cups chicken broth
- 1 ½ cups wild rice

Directions:

1. Season the chicken with salt, onion powder, Cajun seasoning, white pepper, red pepper, and paprika. Warm oil on Sauté in your Instant Pot. Cook celery and pumpkin for 5 minutes; set aside. In the pot, sear chicken for 3 minutes per side until golden brown; reserve.

2. Into the cooker, add ¼ cup chicken stock to deglaze the pan, scrape away any browned bits from the bottom. Add in onion and cook for 2 minutes until fragrant. Take back the celery and pumpkin to the cooker and add the wild rice and remaining chicken stock. Place the chicken over the rice mixture. Seal the lid and cook for 10 minutes on High Pressure. Release the pressure quickly. Place rice and chicken pieces in serving plates and serve.

Fennel Chicken With Tomato Sauce

Servings: 4
Cooking Time: 35 Minutes
Ingredients:

- 1 lb chicken breasts
- ½ cup chicken broth
- Salt and pepper to taste
- 1 tbsp fennel seeds
- 2 tbsp olive oil
- 2 cups tomato-basil sauce

Directions:

1. Place the chicken breasts, olive oil, chicken broth, fennel seeds, salt, and pepper in your Instant Pot. Seal the lid, select Manual, and cook for 20 minutes on High pressure. When done, perform a quick pressure release and unlock the lid. Shred the chicken and add in tomato sauce. Simmer for 5 minutes on Saute. Serve immediately.

Rosemary Chicken With Asparagus Sauce

Servings: 4
Cooking Time: 40 Minutes
Ingredients:

- 1 whole chicken
- 4 garlic cloves, minced
- 2 tbsp olive oil
- 4 fresh thyme, minced
- 3 fresh rosemary, minced
- 2 lemons, zested, quartered
- Salt and pepper to taste
- 2 tbsp olive oil
- 8 oz asparagus, chopped
- 1 onion, chopped
- 1 cup chicken stock
- 1 tbsp soy sauce
- 1 fresh thyme sprig
- 1 tbsp flour
- Chopped parsley to garnish

Directions:

1. Rub all sides of the chicken with garlic, rosemary, black pepper, lemon zest, thyme, and salt. Into the chicken cavity, insert lemon wedges. Warm the olive oil on Sauté in your Instant Pot. Add in onion and asparagus, and sauté for 5 minutes until softened. Mix chicken stock, thyme sprig, black pepper, soy sauce, and salt. Into the inner pot, set trivet over asparagus mixture.

2. On top of the trivet, place the chicken with breast-side up. Seal the lid, select Manual, and cook for 20 minutes on High. Do a quick release. Remove the chicken

to a serving platter. In the inner pot, sprinkle flour over asparagus mixture and blend the sauce with an immersion blender until desired consistency. Top the chicken with asparagus sauce and garnish with parsley.

Chicken Salad

Servings: 6
Cooking Time: 15 Minutes
Ingredients:
- 1 cup chicken broth
- 2 pounds boneless, skinless chicken breasts
- 2 medium stalks celery, diced
- 1 cup chopped pecans
- 1 ½ cups mayonnaise
- 1 tablespoon Dijon mustard
- ½ teaspoon salt
- ¼ teaspoon ground black pepper

Directions:
1. Add broth and chicken to the Instant Pot. Lock lid.
2. Press the Manual or Pressure Cook button and adjust time to 15 minutes. When timer beeps, let pressure release naturally for 10 minutes. Quick-release any additional pressure until float valve drops. Unlock lid. Check chicken using a meat thermometer to ensure the internal temperature is at least 165°F.
3. Using two forks, pull apart chicken in pot.
4. Using a slotted spoon, transfer chicken to a large bowl. Stir in remaining ingredients. Refrigerate until chilled. Serve.

Savory Orange Chicken

Servings: 6
Cooking Time: 25 Minutes
Ingredients:
- 2 tbsp olive oil
- 6 chicken breasts, cubed
- 1/3 cup chicken stock
- ¼ cup soy sauce
- 2 tbsp brown sugar
- 1 tbsp lemon juice
- 1 tbsp garlic powder
- 1 tsp chili sauce
- 1 cup orange juice
- Salt and pepper to taste
- 1 tbsp cornstarch

Directions:

1. Warm oil on Sauté in your Instant Pot. Sear the chicken for 5 minutes until browned, stirring occasionally. Set aside in a bowl. In the pot, mix orange juice, chicken stock, sugar, chili sauce, garlic powder, lemon juice, and soy sauce. Stir in chicken to coat. Seal the lid.
2. Cook on High Pressure for 7 minutes. Release the pressure quickly. Take ¼ cup liquid from the pot to a bowl and stir in cornstarch to dissolve. Pour the sauce in the pot and stir until the color is consistent. Press Sauté and cook the sauce for 2-3 minutes until thickened. Season with pepper and salt. Serve warm.

Cumin Chicken With Capers

Servings: 4
Cooking Time: 30 Minutes
Ingredients:
- 4 chicken breasts
- ½ cup butter
- ½ tsp cumin
- Salt and pepper to taste
- Juice of 1 lemon
- 1 cup chicken broth
- ½ cup capers

Directions:
1. Melt butter in your Instant Pot on Sauté. Sprinkle chicken breasts with cumin, salt, and pepper and place in the pot. Cook for 7-8 minutes on all sides. Stir in lemon juice, chicken broth, and capers and seal the lid. Select Manual and cook for 10 minutes on High pressure. Once ready, allow a natural release for 5 minutes and unlock the lid.

Crispy Bacon & Bean Chicken

Servings: 4
Cooking Time: 65 Minutes
Ingredients:
- 4 boneless, skinless chicken thighs
- 1 cup shredded Monterey Jack cheese
- 2 tbsp olive oil
- 4 slices bacon, crumbled
- 1 onion, diced
- 4 garlic cloves, minced
- 1 tbsp tomato paste
- 1 tbsp oregano
- 1 tbsp ground cumin
- 1 tsp chili powder

- ½ tsp cayenne pepper
- 1 can tomatoes
- 1 cup chicken broth
- 1 tsp salt
- 1 cup cooked corn
- 1 red bell pepper, chopped
- 15 oz red kidney beans
- 2 tbsp chopped cilantro

Directions:

1. Warm oil on Sauté in your Instant Pot. Sear the chicken for 3 minutes for each side until browned. Set aside. In the same oil, fry bacon until crispy, about 5 minutes; set aside. Add in onion and cook for 3 minutes until fragrant. Stir in garlic, oregano, cayenne, cumin, tomato paste, bell pepper, and chili and cook for 30 more seconds.

2. Pour in the broth, salt, and tomatoes. Bring to a boil. Take back the chicken and bacon to the pot and ensure it is submerged in the braising liquid. Seal the lid and cook on High Pressure for 15 minutes. Release the pressure quickly. Pour the corn and kidney beans into the cooker, Press Sauté and bring the liquid to a boil; cook for 10 minutes. Serve topped with shredded cheese and cilantro.

Chicken Fricassee

Servings: 4
Cooking Time: 40 Minutes
Ingredients:

- 4 chicken breasts
- 2 tbsp olive oil
- 1 onion, chopped
- 2 garlic cloves, minced
- Salt and pepper to taste
- ½ cup dry white wine
- ½ cup chicken broth
- ¼ cup heavy cream
- 2 tbsp capers
- 1 bay leaf
- 2 tbsp tarragon, chopped

Directions:

1. Warm the olive oil in your Instant Pot on Sauté. Sprinkle chicken with salt and pepper and place in the pot. Cook for 6 minutes on all sides. Add in onion and garlic and cook for 3 minutes. Pour in chicken broth, white wine, and bay leaf. Seal the lid, select Manual, and cook for 15 minutes on High pressure.

2. When ready, perform a quick pressure release. Remove bay leaf and put in heavy cream and capers. Stir for 2-3 minutes and cook in the residual heat until thoroughly warmed. Ladle into bowls, top with tarragon, and serve.

Tasty Indian Chicken Curry

Servings: 6
Cooking Time: 30 Minutes
Ingredients:

- 1 can coconut milk, refrigerated overnight
- 2 lb boneless, skinless chicken legs
- 2 tbsp butter
- 1 large onion, minced
- 1 tbsp grated fresh ginger
- 1 tbsp minced fresh garlic
- ½ tsp ground turmeric
- 1 tbsp Kashmiri chili powder
- 3 tomatoes, pureed
- 2 tbsp Indian curry paste
- 2 tbsp dried fenugreek
- 1 tsp garam masala
- Salt to taste

Directions:

1. Melt butter on Sauté in your Instant Pot. Add in onion and cook for 3 minutes until fragrant. Stir in ginger, turmeric, garlic, and red chili powder for 2 minutes. Place the water from the coconut milk can in a bowl and mix with pureed tomatoes and chicken. Pour in the onion mixture.

2. Seal the lid and cook on High Pressure for 8 minutes. Release the pressure quickly. Stir in coconut milk, fenugreek, salt, curry paste, and garam masala. Simmer for 10 minutes until the sauce thickens on Sauté. Serve.

Spicy Ground Turkey Chili With Vegetables

Servings: 6
Cooking Time: 60 Minutes
Ingredients:

- 1 tbsp olive oil
- 1 small onion, diced
- 2 garlic cloves, minced
- 1 lb ground turkey
- 2 bell peppers, chopped
- 6 potatoes, chopped

- 1 cup carrots, chopped
- 1 cup corn kernels, roasted
- 1 cup tomato puree
- 1 cup diced tomatoes
- 1 cup chicken broth
- 1 tbsp ground cumin
- 1 tbsp chili powder
- Salt and pepper to taste

Directions:

1. Warm oil on Sauté in your Instant Pot and stir-fry onion and garlic until soft for about 3 minutes. Stir in turkey and cook until thoroughly browned, about 5-6 minutes. Add the bell peppers, potatoes, carrots, corn, tomato puree, tomatoes, broth, cumin, chili powder, salt, and pepper, and stir to combine. Seal the lid and cook for 25 minutes on High Pressure. Do a quick release. Set to Sauté and cook uncovered for 15 more minutes. Serve.

Chicken & Quinoa Soup

Servings: 6
Cooking Time: 30 Minutes

Ingredients:

- 2 tbsp butter
- 1 cup red onion, chopped
- 1 cup carrots, chopped
- 1 cup celery, chopped
- 2 chicken breasts, cubed
- 4 cups chicken broth
- 6 oz quinoa, rinsed
- 2 tbsp parsley, chopped
- Salt and pepper to taste
- 4 oz mascarpone cheese
- 1 cup milk
- 1 cup heavy cream

Directions:

1. Melt butter on Sauté in your Instant Pot. Add carrots, onion, and celery and cook for 5 minutes. Add in broth, parsley, quinoa, and chicken. Season with pepper and salt. Seal the lid. Cook on High Pressure for 10 minutes. Release the pressure quickly. Add mascarpone to the soup and stir to melt it completely. Stir in heavy cream and milk until the soup is thickened and creamy.

Indian-style Chicken

Servings: 6
Cooking Time: 37 Minutes + Marinating Time

Ingredients:

- 6 chicken thighs, bone-in
- ½ cup Greek yogurt
- 1 tbsp curry paste
- 1 tbsp lemon juice
- Salt and pepper to taste
- 1 tbsp fresh ginger, grated
- 2 tbsp cilantro, chopped

Directions:

1. Combine yogurt, lemon juice, curry paste, salt, and pepper in a bowl. Add in chicken thighs and toss to coat. Let marinate in the fridge for 2 hours. Place the chicken, marinade, ginger, and 1 cup of water in your Instant Pot. Seal the lid, select Manual, and cook for 12 minutes on High pressure. When over, allow a natural release for 10 minutes and unlock the lid. Transfer to a baking tray and put under the broiler 3-5 minutes. Top with cilantro.

Herby Chicken With Peach Gravy

Servings: 4
Cooking Time: 55 Minutes

Ingredients:

- 4 chicken breasts
- ¼ cup olive oil
- 1 cup onions, chopped
- 2 celery stalks, chopped
- 2 peaches, cut into chunks
- ½ tsp dried thyme
- ½ tsp dried sage
- 2 cups chicken stock
- Salt and pepper to taste

Directions:

1. Heat oil on Sauté in your Instant Pot and stir-fry the onions for 2-3 minutes until soft. Add celery stalks and peaches and cook for 5 minutes, stirring occasionally.

2. Rub the meat with salt, pepper, thyme, and sage. Add it to the pot along with the stock. Seal the lid and cook on High Pressure for 35 minutes. Do a quick release. Serve.

Chicken Drumsticks In Sriracha Sauce

Servings: 4
Cooking Time: 20 Minutes
Ingredients:
- 4 boneless, skinless chicken drumsticks
- ½ cup soy sauce
- ½ cup chicken broth
- 3 tbsp honey
- 2 tbsp tomato paste
- 1 tbsp sriracha
- 1-inch piece ginger, grated
- 3 garlic cloves, grated
- 1 tbsp cornstarch
- 1 tbsp water
- 2 tbsp toasted sesame seeds
- 1 tbsp sesame oil
- 2 cups canned black beans
- 2 green onions, chopped

Directions:
1. In your Instant Pot, mix soy sauce, honey, ginger, tomato paste, chicken broth, sriracha, and garlic. Stir until smooth; toss in chicken to coat. Seal the lid and cook for 3 minutes on High Pressure. Release the pressure quickly.
2. Open the lid and press Sauté. In a small bowl, mix water and cornstarch until no lumps remain, stir into the sauce and cook for 5 minutes until thickened. Stir sesame oil and 1½ tablespoons sesame seeds through the chicken mixture; garnish with extra sesame seeds and green onions. Serve with black beans.

Easy Pesto Chicken And Red Potatoes

Servings: 8
Cooking Time: 10 Minutes
Ingredients:
- 3 pounds boneless chicken thighs
- ¾ cup pesto
- 2 pounds red potatoes, quartered
- 1 large sweet onion, peeled and chopped
- 1 cup chicken broth

Directions:
1. Place chicken in a bowl or plastic bag. Add pesto. Toss or shake chicken to distribute the pesto evenly over the thighs. Set aside in the refrigerator.
2. Layer potatoes and onions in the Instant Pot. Pour in the chicken broth. Place chicken on top. Lock lid.
3. Press the Manual button and adjust time to 10 minutes. When timer beeps, let pressure release naturally for 10 minutes. Quick-release any additional pressure until float valve drops and then unlock lid. Check the chicken using a meat thermometer to ensure the internal temperature is at least 165°F.
4. Using a slotted spoon, remove chicken and potatoes and transfer to a platter. Discard liquid. Serve warm.

Sweet & Spicy Bbq Chicken

Servings: 4
Cooking Time: 35 Minutes
Ingredients:
- 6 chicken drumsticks
- 1 tbsp olive oil
- 1 onion, chopped
- 1 tsp garlic, minced
- 1 jalapeño pepper, minced
- ½ cup sweet BBQ sauce
- 1 tbsp arrowroot

Directions:
1. Warm the olive oil in your Instant Pot on Sauté. Add in the onion and cook for 3 minutes. Add in garlic and jalapeño pepper and cook for another minute. Stir in barbecue sauce and 1/2 cup of water. Put in chicken drumsticks and seal the lid. Select Manual and cook for 18 minutes on High pressure. When over, perform a quick pressure release and unlock the lid. Mix 2 tbsp of water and arrowroot and pour it into the pot. Cook for 5 minutes on Sauté until the liquid thickens. Top with sauce and serve.

Best Italian Chicken Balls

Servings: 4
Cooking Time: 35 Minutes
Ingredients:
- 1/3 cup blue cheese, crumbled
- ¼ cup Pecorino Romano cheese, shredded
- 1 lb ground chicken
- 3 tbsp red hot sauce
- 1 egg
- ¼ cup breadcrumbs

- 1 tbsp ranch dressing
- 1 tbsp fresh basil, chopped
- Salt and pepper to taste
- 15 oz canned tomato sauce
- 1 cup chicken broth
- 2 tbsp olive oil

Directions:

1. In a bowl, mix ground chicken, egg, Pecorino cheese, pepper, salt, ranch dressing, blue cheese, hot sauce, and breadcrumbs. Shape the mixture into balls. Warm oil on Sauté in your Instant Pot. Add in the meatballs and cook for 2-3 minutes until browned on all sides.

2. Add in tomato sauce and broth. Seal the lid and cook on High Pressure for 7 minutes. Release the pressure quickly. Remove meatballs carefully and place them on a serving plate. Top with basil and serve.

Chicken Alla Diavola

Servings: 4
Cooking Time: 20 Minutes
Ingredients:

- 1 teaspoon sea salt
- 2 cloves garlic, minced
- 2 tablespoons apple cider vinegar
- 4 tablespoons olive oil, divided
- 1 teaspoon sriracha
- 1 teaspoon chili powder
- ¼ teaspoon cayenne pepper
- 1 pound boneless, skinless chicken breast, cut in 1" cubes
- 2 cups water

Directions:

1. In a medium bowl, whisk together salt, garlic, vinegar, 2 tablespoons oil, sriracha, chili powder, and cayenne pepper. Toss chicken into mixture and coat evenly. Cover and refrigerate for 1 hour.

2. Press the Sauté button on the Instant Pot. Heat remaining 2 tablespoons oil and add the chicken pieces. Stir-fry for about 4 minutes or until browned on all sides. Remove chicken and set aside.

3. Insert trivet into Instant Pot. Add water. Transfer chicken to a large square of aluminum foil. Set the foil onto the trivet. Lock lid.

4. Press the Poultry button and cook for the default time of 15 minutes. When timer beeps, let pressure release naturally for 10 minutes. Quick-release any additional pressure until float valve drops and then unlock lid. Check the chicken using a meat thermometer to ensure the internal temperature is at least 165°F. Serve warm.

Chicken With Honey-lime Sauce

Servings: 4
Cooking Time: 30 Minutes
Ingredients:

- 4 chicken breasts, cut into chunks
- 1 onion, diced
- 4 garlic cloves, smashed
- 1 tbsp honey
- 3 tbsp soy sauce
- 2 tbsp lime juice
- 2 tsp sesame oil
- 1 tsp rice vinegar
- 1 tbsp cornstarch
- Salt and pepper to taste

Directions:

1. Mix garlic, onion, and chicken in your Instant Pot. In a bowl, combine honey, sesame oil, lime juice, soy sauce, and rice vinegar. Pour over the chicken mixture. Seal the lid and cook on High Pressure for 15 minutes. Release the pressure quickly. Mix 1 tbsp water and cornstarch until well dissolved; Stir into the sauce, add salt and pepper to taste. Press Sauté. Simmer the sauce and cook for 2 to 3 minutes as you stir until thickened.

Chicken & Vegetable Stew

Servings: 4
Cooking Time: 45 Minutes
Ingredients:

- 2 cups fire-roasted tomatoes, diced
- ½ cup button mushrooms, sliced
- 1 lb chicken breasts, chopped
- 1 tbsp fresh basil, chopped
- 2 cups coconut milk
- 1 cup chicken broth
- Salt and pepper to taste
- 2 tbsp tomato paste
- 2 celery stalks, chopped
- 2 carrots, chopped
- 2 tbsp coconut oil
- 1 onion, finely chopped

Directions:

1. Warm the coconut oil in your Instant Pot on Sauté. Add celery, onion, and carrots and cook for 7 minutes, stirring constantly. Add tomato paste, basil, and mushrooms. Continue to cook for 10 more minutes. Addin the tomatoes, chicken, coconut milk, chicken broth, salt, and pepper. Seal the lid and cook on Manual for 15 minutes on High. Do a quick release. Serve warm.

Buttermilk Cornish Game Hens

Servings:2
Cooking Time: 15 Minutes
Ingredients:
- 2 Cornish game hens
- 2 cups buttermilk
- 2 tablespoons Italian seasoning
- 2 teaspoons chili powder
- 1 teaspoon salt
- ½ teaspoon ground black pepper
- 1 medium orange, quartered
- 1 ½ cups water
- 1 tablespoon olive oil

Directions:
1. Pat down Cornish game hens with a paper towel. Set aside.
2. In a large bowl, whisk together buttermilk, Italian seasoning, chili powder, salt, and pepper. Place hens in mixture. Refrigerate covered overnight.
3. Place orange quarters in cavities of hens.
4. Add water to the Instant Pot. Insert steamer basket and place hens in basket. Lock lid.
5. Press the Meat button and adjust time to 10 minutes. When timer beeps, let pressure release naturally for 5 minutes. Quick-release any additional pressure until float valve drops. Unlock lid. Check hens using a meat thermometer to ensure internal temperature is at least 165°F.
6. Transfer hens to a parchment paper–lined baking sheet and brush hens with oil. Remove and discard orange quarters from cavities of hens. Broil 5 minutes.
7. Transfer hens to a serving dish. Serve warm.

Creamy Mascarpone Chicken

Servings: 4
Cooking Time: 30 Minutes
Ingredients:
- 8 bacon slices, cooked and crumbled
- 1 lb chicken breasts
- 8 oz mascarpone cheese
- 1 tbsp Dijon mustard
- 1 tsp ranch seasoning
- 3 tbsp cornstarch
- ½ cup cheddar, shredded

Directions:
1. Place the chicken breasts, mustard, and mascarpone cheese in your Instant Pot. Add in ranch seasoning and 1 cup of water. Seal the lid, select Manual, and cook for 15 minutes on High pressure. Once ready, perform a quick pressure release and unlock the lid. Remove the chicken and shred it. Add in cornstarch, shredded chicken, cheese, and bacon and cook for 3 minutes on Sauté. Lock the lid and let chill for a few minutes. Serve.

Insalata Caprese Chicken Bowls

Servings:4
Cooking Time: 5 Minutes
Ingredients:
- 1 ½ pounds boneless, skinless chicken breasts, cut into 1" cubes
- 1 can diced tomatoes, including juice
- ½ teaspoon salt
- ½ teaspoon ground black pepper
- 1 container fresh ciliegine mozzarella, drained and halved
- 1 tablespoon olive oil
- 2 tablespoons balsamic vinegar
- ½ cup julienned fresh basil leaves

Directions:
1. In the Instant Pot, add chicken and tomatoes. Lock lid.
2. Press the Manual or Pressure Cook button and adjust time to 5 minutes. When timer beeps, let pressure release naturally for 10 minutes. Quick-release any additional pressure until float valve drops. Unlock lid. Check chicken using a meat thermometer to ensure internal temperature is at least 165°F.
3. Using a slotted spoon, transfer chicken and tomatoes to four bowls. Season with salt and pepper. Add mozzarella halves. Drizzle with oil and balsamic vinegar. Garnish with basil. Serve immediately.

Tasty Chicken Breasts With Bbq Sauce

Servings: 6
Cooking Time: 20 Minutes
Ingredients:
- 2 lb chicken breasts
- 1 tsp salt
- 1 ½ cups barbecue sauce
- 1 small onion, minced
- 1 cup carrots, chopped
- 4 garlic cloves

Directions:

1. Rub salt onto the chicken and place it in the Instant Pot. Add onion, carrots, garlic, and barbeque sauce; toss to coat. Seal the lid, press Manual, and cook on High for 15 minutes. Do a quick release. Shred the chicken and stir into the sauce. Serve.

Pork, Beef & Lamb

Spiced Pork With Orange & Cinnamon

Servings: 4
Cooking Time: 70 Minutes
Ingredients:
- 2 tbsp olive oil
- 2 lb pork shoulder
- 1 cinnamon stick
- 1 cup orange juice
- 1 tbsp cumin
- ½ tsp garlic powder
- ¼ tsp onion powder
- 1 onion, chopped
- 1 jalapeño pepper, diced
- 2 tsp thyme
- ½ tsp oregano
- Salt and pepper to taste

Directions:
1. Place half of the oil in a small bowl. Add cumin, garlic powder, onion powder, thyme, oregano, salt, and pepper and stir well to combine the mixture. Rub it all over the meat, making sure that the pork is well-coated. Heat the remaining oil on Sauté. Add the pork and sear it on all sides until browned. Transfer to a plate. Pour the orange juice into the pan and deglaze the bottom with a spatula.
2. Add cinnamon stick, onion, and jalapeño and stir to combine well. Return the pork to the pot. Seal the lid, select Pressure Cook, and cook for 40 minutes. When ready, allow for a natural pressure release for about 10 minutes. Grab two forks and shred the pork inside the pot. Stir to combine with the juices and serve.

Green Pea & Beef Ragout

Servings: 4
Cooking Time: 25 Minutes
Ingredients:
- 2 lb beef, tender cuts, cut into bits
- 2 cups green peas
- 1 onion, diced
- 1 tomato, diced
- 3 cups beef broth
- ½ cup tomato paste
- 1 tsp cayenne pepper
- 1 tbsp flour
- 1 tsp salt
- ½ tsp dried thyme
- ½ tsp red pepper flakes

Directions:
1. Add beef, green peas, onion, tomato, broth, tomato paste, cayenne pepper, flour, salt, thyme, and red pepper flakes to the Instant Pot. Seal the lid, press Manual/Pressure Cook and cook for 10 minutes on High Pressure. When done, release the steam naturally for 10 minutes. Serve.

Shroomy Meatballs

Servings: 4
Cooking Time: 16 Minutes
Ingredients:
- ½ pound ground pork
- ½ pound 80/20 ground beef
- ½ can condensed cream of mushroom soup
- 1 large egg, lightly beaten
- 1 cup panko bread crumbs
- ½ teaspoon salt
- ½ teaspoon ground black pepper
- 2 tablespoons olive oil
- 2 cups water

Directions:
1. In a medium bowl, combine pork, beef, soup, egg, bread crumbs, salt, and pepper. Form into eight meatballs. Set aside.
2. Press the Sauté button on the Instant Pot and heat oil. Place meatballs around the edge of pot. Sear all sides of meatballs, about 4 minutes total. Press the Cancel button.
3. Transfer seared meatballs to a 7-cup glass baking dish. Discard extra juice and oil from pot.
4. Add water to the Instant Pot and insert steam rack. Place glass baking dish on top of steam rack. Lock lid.
5. Press the Manual or Pressure Cook button and adjust time to 12 minutes. When timer beeps, let pressure release naturally for 10 minutes. Quick-release any additional pressure until float valve drops. Unlock lid.
6. Transfer meatballs to plates. Serve warm.

Carnitas Lettuce Wraps

Servings: 6
Cooking Time: 60 Minutes
Ingredients:
- 1 tablespoon unsweetened cocoa powder
- 2 teaspoons salt
- 1 teaspoon cayenne pepper
- 2 teaspoons ground oregano
- 1 teaspoon white pepper
- 1 teaspoon garlic powder
- 1 teaspoon onion salt
- 1 teaspoon ground cumin
- ½ teaspoon ground coriander
- 1 pork shoulder
- 2 tablespoons olive oil
- 2–3 cups water
- 1 head butter lettuce, washed and dried
- 1 small jalapeño, sliced
- ¼ cup julienned radishes
- 1 medium avocado, diced
- 2 small Roma tomatoes, diced
- 2 limes, cut into wedges

Directions:
1. In a small bowl, combine cocoa powder, salt, cayenne pepper, oregano, white pepper, garlic powder, onion salt, cumin, and coriander. Massage seasoning into pork shoulder and refrigerate covered overnight.
2. Press the Sauté button on the Instant Pot. Add 2 tablespoons oil. Sear roast on all sides ensuring all sides are browned, about 8–10 minutes. Add enough water to almost cover the meat. Lock lid.
3. Press the Manual button and adjust time to 45 minutes. When timer beeps, let pressure release naturally for 10 minutes. Quick-release any additional pressure until float valve drops and then unlock lid.
4. Transfer pork to a platter. Using two forks, shred the meat. Discard all but ½ cup of cooking liquid. Add meat back into Instant Pot. Press the Sauté button and stir-fry meat for 4–5 minutes creating some crispy edges.
5. Serve with lettuce leaves, jalapeño slices, radishes, avocado, tomatoes, and lime wedges.

Carrot Casserole With Beef & Potato

Servings: 3
Cooking Time: 20 Minutes
Ingredients:
- 1 lb lean beef, with bones
- 2 carrots
- 1 potato, sliced
- 3 tbsp olive oil
- ½ tsp salt

Directions:
1. Mix beef, carrots, potato, olive oil, and salt in the Instant Pot. Pour enough water to cover and seal the lid. Cook on High Pressure for 15 minutes. Do a quick release and serve hot.

Beef Arancini With Potatoes

Servings: 4
Cooking Time: 40 Minutes
Ingredients:
- 1 lb lean ground beef
- 6 oz rice
- 2 onions, peeled, chopped
- 2 garlic cloves, crushed
- 1 egg, beaten
- 1 potato peeled, chopped
- 3 tbsp olive oil
- 1 tsp salt

Directions:
1. In a bowl, combine beef, rice, onions, garlic, egg, and salt. Shape the mixture into 15-16 meatballs. Grease the inner pot with 1 tbsp of olive oil. Press Sauté and cook the meatballs for 3-4 minutes, or until slightly brown.
2. Remove the meatballs. Add the remaining oil and make a layer of potato. Top with meatballs, cover with water, and seal the lid. Adjust the release steam handle. Cook on Meat/Stew for 15 minutes on High. Do a quick release.

Seasoned Boneless Pork Loin

Servings: 4
Cooking Time: 14 Minutes
Ingredients:
- 1 teaspoon salt
- 1 teaspoon ground black pepper
- 1 teaspoon Italian seasoning
- 2 tablespoons all-purpose flour
- 1 tablespoon grated Parmesan cheese
- 2 boneless pork loin chops
- 2 tablespoons olive oil

- 1 cup water

Directions:

1. In a large bowl, combine salt, pepper, Italian seasoning, flour, and cheese. Coat chops in mixture. Set aside.
2. Press the Sauté button on the Instant Pot and heat oil. Add chops to pot and sear 2 minutes on each side, for a total of 8 minutes. Press the Cancel button. Remove pork from pot and set aside.
3. Pour water into the Instant Pot. Place chops in steamer basket and insert into pot. Lock lid.
4. Press the Manual or Pressure Cook button and adjust time to 6 minutes. When timer beeps, quick-release pressure until float valve drops. Unlock lid.
5. Transfer chops to a cutting board. Let rest 5 minutes before slicing. Serve warm.

Italian Meatballs With Pomodoro Sauce

Servings: 6
Cooking Time: 25 Minutes

Ingredients:

- ¾ cup grated Parmigiano-Reggiano cheese
- 1 ½ lb ground beef
- 1/3 cup warm water
- ½ cup bread crumbs
- 1 egg
- 2 tbsp fresh parsley
- ¼ tsp garlic powder
- ¼ tsp dried oregano
- Salt and pepper to taste
- ½ cup capers
- 1 tsp olive oil
- 3 cups marinara sauce

Directions:

1. In a bowl, mix ground beef, parsley, garlic powder, pepper, oregano, crumbs, egg, and salt; shape into meatballs. Warm oil on Sauté. Add meatballs to the oil and brown for 2-3 minutes and all sides. Pour in water and marinara and stir. Seal the lid and cook on High Pressure for 10 minutes. Release the pressure quickly. Serve topped with capers and cheese.

Korean Short Ribs

Servings:6
Cooking Time: 25 Minutes

Ingredients:

- ½ cup soy sauce
- ½ cup pure maple syrup
- ½ cup rice wine
- 1 tablespoon sesame oil
- 1 teaspoon white pepper
- ½ teaspoon ground ginger
- ½ teaspoon garlic powder
- ½ teaspoon gochujang
- 3 pounds beef short ribs
- 1 cup beef broth
- 2 green onions, sliced
- 1 tablespoon toasted sesame seeds

Directions:

1. In a small bowl, combine soy sauce, maple syrup, rice wine, sesame oil, white pepper, ground ginger, garlic powder, and gochujang. Using your hands, rub this mixture into the rib sections. Refrigerate covered for 60 minutes up to overnight.
2. Add beef broth to Instant Pot. Insert trivet. Arrange ribs standing upright with the meaty side facing outward. Lock lid.
3. Press the Manual button and adjust time to 25 minutes. When the timer beeps, let pressure release naturally until float valve drops and then unlock lid.
4. Transfer ribs to a serving platter and garnish with green onions and sesame seeds.

Vegetable Casserole With Smoked Bacon

Servings: 4
Cooking Time: 30 Minutes

Ingredients:

- ½ lb smoked bacon, chopped
- ½ cup carrots, sliced
- 1 cup vegetable stock
- ¾ cup half and half
- 4 golden potatoes, peeled and chopped
- 4 endives, chopped
- Salt and pepper to taste

Directions:

1. Set to Sauté and add the bacon. Cook for 2 minutes until slightly crispy. Add the potatoes, carrots, 2 cups water, and vegetable stock. Seal the lid and cook for 10 minutes on High Pressure. Release the pressure quickly.

Add the endives and cook for 5 more minutes on Sauté. Stir in the half and half and season with salt and pepper. Cook for 3 more minutes. Serve.

T-bone Steaks With Basil & Mustard

Servings: 4

Cooking Time: 40 Minutes + Marinating Time

Ingredients:

- 1 lb T-bone steak
- Salt and pepper to taste
- 2 tbsp Dijon mustard
- ¼ cup oil
- ½ tsp dried basil, crushed

Directions:

1. Whisk together oil, mustard, salt, pepper, and basil. Brush each steak and Refrigerate for 1 hour. Then, insert a steamer tray in the Instant Pot. Pour in 1 cup of water and arrange the steaks on the tray. Seal the lid and cook on Manual for 25 minutes on High. Do a quick release. Discard the liquid, remove the tray, and hit Sauté. Brown the steaks for 5 minutes, turning once.

Spicy Lamb & Bean Chili

Servings: 4

Cooking Time: 53 Minutes

Ingredients:

- 1 cup chopped green chilies
- 1 cup cannellini beans, soaked
- 1 lb ground lamb
- 2 tbsp olive oil
- 1 onion, chopped
- ½ tbsp chili powder
- ½ tsp cayenne pepper
- 1 tsp cumin
- 1 tsp fennel seeds
- 1 can diced tomatoes
- 1 tbsp tomato paste
- 3 cups chicken broth
- Salt and pepper to taste

Directions:

1. Warm the olive oil in your Instant Pot on Sauté. Add in ground lamb and cook for 5 minutes until mostly brown. Stir in onion, chili powder, cayenne pepper, cumin, fennel seeds, salt, and pepper and sauté for 3 minutes.

2. Pour in tomatoes, tomato paste, green chilies, cannellini beans, and chicken broth and seal the lid. Select Manual and cook for 25 minutes on High.

3. When ready, allow a natural release for 10 minutes and unlock the lid. Serve with sour cream.

Vegetable & Lamb Casserole

Servings: 4

Cooking Time: 50 Minutes

Ingredients:

- 1 lb lamb stew meat, cubed
- 2 tbsp olive oil
- 1 onion, chopped
- 3 garlic cloves, minced
- 2 tomatoes, chopped
- ½ lb baby potatoes
- ½ lb green beans, chopped
- 1 carrot, chopped
- 1 onion, chopped
- 1 celery stalk, chopped
- 2 tbsp white wine
- 2 cups lamb stock
- 1 tsp Hungarian paprika
- 1 tsp cumin, ground
- ¼ tsp oregano, dried
- ¼ tsp rosemary, dried
- Salt and pepper to taste

Directions:

1. Warm the olive oil in your Instant Pot on Sauté. Add in lamb cubes and cook for 5-6 minutes until no longer pink. Stir in onion and garlic and sauté for another 3 minutes. Pour in tomatoes, potatoes, green beans, carrot, onion, celery, white wine, lamb stock, paprika, cumin, oregano, rosemary, salt, and pepper and seal the lid. Select Manual and cook for 20 minutes on High pressure. When over, allow a natural release for 10 minutes and unlock the lid.

Mongolian Beef Bbq

Servings:4

Cooking Time: 20 Minutes

Ingredients:

- 1 tablespoon sesame oil
- 1 skirt steak, sliced into thin strips
- ¼ cup coconut aminos
- ½ cup pure maple syrup

- 1" knob of fresh gingerroot, peeled and grated
- 4 cloves garlic, minced
- ½ cup plus 2 tablespoons water, divided
- 2 tablespoons arrowroot powder

Directions:
1. Press the Sauté button on the Instant Pot. Heat oil and cook steak strips until barely seared on all sides, about 2–3 minutes.
2. In a medium bowl, whisk together coconut aminos, maple syrup, ginger, garlic, and ½ cup water. Pour over beef and stir to deglaze any bits around the edges and bottom of the Instant Pot. Lock lid.
3. Press the Manual button and adjust time to 10 minutes. When timer beeps, quick-release pressure until float valve drops and then unlock lid.
4. In a small dish, whisk together arrowroot and 2 tablespoons water until smooth to create a slurry. Stir this mixture into the beef mixture. Press Sauté button, press Adjust button to change the temperature to Less, and simmer unlidded for 5 minutes until the sauce thickens.
5. Ladle mixture into bowls and serve.

Vietnamese-style Rice Noodle Soup

Servings: 4
Cooking Time: 1 Hour 10 Minutes
Ingredients:
- 2 tbsp coconut oil
- 1 yellow onion, quartered
- ¼ cup minced fresh ginger
- 2 tsp coriander seeds
- 2 lb beef neck bones
- Salt and pepper to taste
- 8 oz rice noodles
- ¼ tbsp sugar
- 2 tbsp fish sauce
- 10 oz sirloin steak
- 2 tbsp cilantro, chopped
- 2 scallions, chopped
- 2 jalapeño peppers, minced
- 2 cups Swiss chard, chopped
- 1 red onion, chopped

Directions:
1. Warm coconut oil on Sauté. Add ginger and yellow onion and cook for 4 minutes. Stir in coriander seeds for 1 minute. Add in beef meat, bones, 4 cups of water, and salt. Seal the lid and cook on High Pressure for 30 minutes. Release the pressure naturally for 10 minutes. Transfer the meat to a bowl to cool slightly. Pat the beef dry with paper towels and slice it.
2. In hot water, soak rice noodles for 8 minutes until softened and pliable. Drain and rinse with cold water. Drain the liquid from the cooker into a separate pot through a fine-mesh strainer; get rid of any solids.
3. Add fish sauce and sugar to the broth and pour in the cooker to heat on Sauté. Place the noodles in bowls. Top with beef slices, scallions, swiss chard, jalapeño, cilantro, red onion, and pepper. Spoon the broth over and serve.

Sambal Beef Noodles

Servings: 4
Cooking Time: 65 Minutes
Ingredients:
- 1 lb beef chuck roast, cubed
- 2 tbsp sesame oil
- Salt and pepper to taste
- 1 chopped onion
- 2 minced garlic cloves
- 3 tbsp sambal oelek chili paste
- 2 cups water
- 8 oz egg noodles

Directions:
1. Warm the sesame oil in your Instant Pot on Sauté. Place in the beef roast and cook for 6-7 minutes, stirring often. Add in salt, pepper, onion, sambal oelek chili paste, garlic, and 1 cup of water. Seal the lid, select Manual, and cook for 30 minutes on High pressure.
2. Once done, allow a natural release for 10 minutes, then perform a quick pressure release. Transfer beef roast to a plate. Pour in 1 cup of water in the pot and bring to a boil on Sauté. Add in noodles and cook for 4-5 minutes. Put the beef back to the pot and stir. Serve warm.

Chorizo With Macaroni & Cheddar Cheese

Servings: 6
Cooking Time: 20 Minutes
Ingredients:
- 1 lb macaroni
- 3 oz chorizo, chopped
- 3 cups water
- 1 tbsp garlic powder
- 2 tbsp minced garlic

- 2 cups milk
- 2 cups cheddar, shredded
- Salt to taste

Directions:

1. On Sauté and stir-fry chorizo until crispy for about 6 minutes. Set aside. Wipe the pot with kitchen paper. Add in water, macaroni, garlic, and salt. Seal lid and cook for 5 minutes on High Pressure. Release the pressure quickly. Stir in cheese, garlic powder, and milk until the cheese melts. Top with chorizo and serve.

Pulled Bbq Beef

Servings: 6
Cooking Time: 65 Minutes
Ingredients:

- 3 lb beef chuck roast
- 2 tbsp olive oil
- 1 cup BBQ sauce
- 1 tbsp Dijon mustard
- 1 tsp smoked paprika
- Salt and pepper to taste
- 2 cups beef broth
- 3 tbsp cilantro, chopped

Directions:

1. Warm the olive oil in your Instant Pot on Sauté. Sprinkle beef with salt and pepper and place it in the pot and cook for 8-10 minutes on all sides. Add in BBQ sauce, Dijon mustard, smoked paprika, salt, pepper, and beef broth and seal the lid. Select Manual and cook for 35 minutes on High pressure.

2. Once ready, allow a natural release for 10 minutes, then perform a quick pressure release, and unlock the lid. Remove beef and shred it using 2 forks. Put it back to the pot and mix with the remaining liquid. Top with cilantro and serve.

Quick French-style Lamb With Sesame

Servings: 4
Cooking Time: 45 Minutes
Ingredients:

- 12 oz lamb, tender cuts, ½-inch thick
- 1 cup rice
- 1 cup green peas
- 3 tbsp sesame seeds
- 4 cups beef broth
- 1 tsp salt
- ½ tsp dried thyme
- 3 tbsp butter

Directions:

1. Mix the meat in the pot with broth. Seal the lid and cook on High Pressure for 15 minutes. Do a quick release. Remove the meat but keep the liquid. Add rice and green peas. Season with salt and thyme. Stir well and top with the meat. Seal the lid and cook on Manual for 18 minutes on High. Do a quick release. Carefully unlock the lid. Stir in butter and sesame seeds. Serve immediately.

Tandoori Pork Butt

Servings: 4
Cooking Time: 61 Minutes
Ingredients:

- 2 lb pork butt, boneless, trimmed of excess fat
- 1 tsp ground cumin
- 1 tsp ground coriander
- 1 tsp paprika
- 1 green chili, minced
- 1 tsp garam masala
- 2 tbsp ghee
- 1 onion, chopped
- 2 garlic cloves, minced
- 1-inch piece ginger, grated
- 1 can coconut milk
- Salt and pepper to taste
- Lime wedges for garnish

Directions:

1. Mix the salt, pepper, ground coriander, paprika, cumin, and garam masala in a bowl. Sprinkle pork butt with this mixture. Melt ghee in your Instant Pot on Sauté. Place in green chili, ginger, onion, and garlic and cook for 2 minutes. Add in pork butt and cook for 3-4 minutes.

2. Pour in coconut milk and ½ cup of water and seal the lid. Select Manual and cook for 35 minutes on High pressure. Once ready, allow a natural release for 10 minutes, then perform a quick pressure release, and unlock the lid. Cut the butt into slices and serve with lemon wedges.

Cumin Pork Chops With Peach Sauce

Servings: 4
Cooking Time: 20 Minutes
Ingredients:
- 4 pork chops
- 1 tsp cumin seeds
- Salt and pepper to taste
- 2 cups peaches, sliced
- 1 tbsp vegetable oil
- ¾ cup vegetable stock

Directions:
1. Sprinkle salt, cumin, and pepper on the pork chops. Set to Sauté and warm oil. Add the chops and cook for 3-5 minutes until browned and set aside on a bowl. Arrange peach slices at the bottom of the cooker.
2. Place the pork on top of the peaches. Add any juice from the plate over the pork and apply stock around the edges. Seal lid and cook on High Pressure for 8 minutes. Do a quick pressure release. Transfer the pork to a serving plate and spoon over the peach sauce before serving.

Garlic & Thyme Pork

Servings: 4
Cooking Time: 58 Minutes
Ingredients:
- 1 lb pork brisket
- 2 garlic cloves, minced
- 2 tsp paprika
- 1 tsp ground cumin
- 1 tsp onion powder
- 2 tbsp flour
- 2 tbsp olive oil
- 1 ½ cups chicken broth
- ½ cup red wine
- 6 garlic cloves, minced
- 1 tbsp thyme, chopped
- 1 tbsp butter
- 1 cup mushrooms, sliced
- Salt and pepper to taste

Directions:
1. Mix the onion powder, paprika, cumin, salt, pepper, and garlic in a bowl. Sprinkle pork brisket with this mixture. Cover all brisket with flour. Warm the oil in your Instant Pot on Sauté. Place in brisket and cook for 8 minutes on all sides. Pour in red wine and scrape any brown bits from the bottom. Add in garlic, thyme, and broth and seal the lid. Select Manual and cook for 30 minutes.
2. When ready, allow a natural release for 10 minutes, then perform a quick pressure release, and unlock the lid. Remove brisket to a plate and cooking liquid in a bowl. Melt butter in your Instant Pot on Sauté. Place in mushrooms and cook until they are soft. Pour in reserved liquid and cook for another minute. Cut brisket in slices and top with mushroom sauce. Serve warm.

Cajun Pork Carnitas

Servings: 4
Cooking Time: 65 Minutes
Ingredients:
- 1 lb pork shoulder, trimmed of excess fat
- 3 tbsp olive oil
- 1 onion, chopped
- 1 cup chicken stock
- ½ cup sour cream
- 2 tbsp tomato paste
- 1 tbsp lemon juice
- Salt and pepper to taste
- 1 tsp cayenne pepper
- 1 tsp garlic powder
- 1 tbsp Cajun seasoning
- 4 tortillas, warm

Directions:
1. Warm the olive oil in your Instant Pot on Sauté. Place in the pork and cook for 7-8 minutes on all sides. Stir in onion and cook for 1-2 more minutes. Pour in chicken stock, sour cream, tomato paste, lemon juice, salt, pepper, cayenne pepper, Cajun seasoning, and garlic powder. Seal the lid, select Manual, and cook for 25 minutes on High.
2. When ready, allow a natural release for 10 minutes and unlock the lid. Remove pork and shred it. Put shredded pork back to the pot and cook for 6-8 minutes on Sauté. Serve with warm tortillas.

Apricot Jam-glazed Ham

Servings: 6
Cooking Time: 40 Minutes
Ingredients:
- 4 lb smoked ham
- ¾ cup apricot jam
- ½ cup brown sugar
- Juice from 1 lime
- 2 tsp Dijon mustard
- ½ tsp ground cardamom
- ¼ tsp ground nutmeg
- Black pepper to taste

Directions:
1. Pour 1 cup of water in your Instant Pot and add a trivet. Lay the ham on the trivet. In a bowl, mix the remaining ingredients until the sugar is dissolved. Pour the mixture all over the ham. Seal the lid and cook on High Pressure for 10 minutes. Release the pressure quickly.
2. Transfer the ham to a cutting board. Allow to sit for 10 minutes before slicing. Press Sauté. Simmer the liquid and cook for 4 to 6 minutes until thickened into a sauce. Plate the sliced ham and drizzle with sauce before serving.

Southern Pot Roast With Pepperoncini

Servings: 6
Cooking Time: 1 Hour 30 Minutes
Ingredients:
- 3 tbsp canola oil
- 2 lb chuck roast
- Salt and pepper to taste
- ¼ cup butter
- 1 onion, finely chopped
- 1 tsp onion powder
- 1 tsp garlic powder
- ½ tsp dried thyme
- ½ tsp dried parsley
- 6 cups beef broth
- ½ cup pepperoncini juice
- 10 pepperoncini
- 5 potatoes, peeled, chopped
- 2 bay leaves

Directions:
1. Warm oil on Sauté. Season chuck roast with pepper and salt, then sear in hot oil for 2 to 4 minutes per side until browned. Set aside.
2. Melt butter and cook the onion for 3 minutes until fragrant. Sprinkle with dried parsley, onion powder, dried thyme, and garlic powder and stir for 30 seconds. Stir in bay leaves, broth, pepperoncini juice, potatoes, and pepperoncini.
3. Nestle chuck roast down into the liquid. Seal the lid and cook on High for 60 minutes. Release pressure naturally for about 10 minutes. Set the chuck roast to a cutting board and use two forks to shred. Serve immediately.

Red Wine Beef & Vegetable Hotpot

Servings: 6
Cooking Time: 40 Minutes
Ingredients:
- 2 sweet potatoes, cut into chunks
- 2 lb stewing beef meat
- ¾ cup red wine
- 1 tbsp ghee
- 6 oz tomato paste
- 6 oz baby carrots, chopped
- 1 onion, finely chopped
- ½ tsp salt
- 4 cups beef broth
- ½ cup green peas
- 1 tsp dried thyme
- 3 garlic cloves, crushed

Directions:
1. Heat ghee on Sauté. Add beef and brown for 5-6 minutes. Add onion and garlic, and keep stirring for 3 more minutes. Add the sweet potatoes, wine, tomato paste, carrots, salt, broth, green peas, and thyme and seal the lid. Cook on Meat/Stew for 20 minutes on High Pressure. Do a quick release. Serve.

Classic Pork Goulash

Servings: 4
Cooking Time: 40 Minutes
Ingredients:
- 12 oz pork neck, cut into bite-sized pieces
- 2 tbsp flour
- 2 tbsp vegetable oil
- 2 onions, peeled, chopped

- 1 carrot, chopped
- 1 chopped celery stalk
- 10 oz button mushrooms
- 4 cups beef broth
- 1 chili pepper, chopped
- 1 tbsp cayenne pepper
- Salt and pepper to taste

Directions:

1. Heat oil on Sauté. Add onions and cook for 2 minutes until translucent. Add flour, chili pepper, carrot, celery, cayenne pepper, and continue to cook for 2 minutes, stirring constantly. Add meat, mushrooms, and beef broth. Season with salt and pepper. Seal the lid and cook on Manual for 30 minutes on High Pressure. Do a quick release and serve immediately.

Beef Shawarma Bowls

Servings: 4
Cooking Time: 3 Minutes
Ingredients:

- 1 boneless sirloin, trimmed and sliced into 3" strips
- 2 tablespoons shawarma seasoning mix
- 1 tablespoon olive oil
- 1 cup water
- 3 medium Roma tomatoes, diced
- 1 small red onion, peeled and sliced
- 1 cup hummus

Directions:

1. In a medium bowl, combine sirloin and shawarma seasoning mix. Refrigerate covered 30 minutes.
2. Press the Sauté button on the Instant Pot and heat oil. Place sirloin in pot and stir-fry 2 minutes, then transfer to steamer basket. Press the Cancel button.
3. Add water to the Instant Pot and insert basket. Lock lid.
4. Press the Manual or Pressure Cook button and adjust time to 1 minute. When timer beeps, quick-release pressure until float valve drops. Unlock lid.
5. Transfer beef to bowls and garnish with tomatoes, onion, and hummus. Serve warm.

Eggplant & Beef Stew With Parmesan

Servings: 6
Cooking Time: 70 Minutes
Ingredients:

- 9 oz beef neck, cut into bite-sized pieces
- 2 cups fire-roasted tomatoes
- 1 eggplant, chopped
- ½ tbsp fresh green peas
- 1 tbsp cayenne pepper
- 1 tbsp beef broth
- 4 tbsp olive oil
- 2 tbsp tomato paste
- 1 tbsp ground chili pepper
- ½ tsp salt
- Parmesan, for garnish

Directions:

1. Rub the meat with salt, cayenne, and chili pepper. Grease the Instant Pot with oil and brown the meat for 5-7 minutes or until golden on Sauté. Add tomatoes, eggplant, green peas, broth, and tomato paste and seal the lid. Cook on Meat/Stew for 40 minutes on High. Do a natural release for 10 minutes. Carefully unlock the lid. Serve warm sprinkled with grated Parmesan cheese.

Moroccan Beef & Cherry Stew

Servings: 4
Cooking Time: 1 Hour 20 Minutes
Ingredients:

- 1 ½ lb stewing beef, trimmed
- ¼ cup toasted almonds, slivered
- 2 tbsp olive oil
- 1 onion, chopped
- 1 tsp ground cinnamon
- ½ tsp paprika
- ½ tsp turmeric
- ½ tsp salt
- ¼ tsp ground ginger
- ¼ tsp ground allspice
- 1-star anise
- 1 cup water
- 1 tbsp honey
- 1 cup dried cherries, halved

Directions:

1. Set the Instant Pot to Sauté and warm olive oil. Add in onion and cook for 3 minutes. Mix in beef and cook for 2 minutes each side until browned. Stir in anise, cinnamon, turmeric, allspice, salt, paprika, and ginger; cook for 2 minutes until aromatic. Add in honey and

water. Seal the lid, press Meat/Stew, and cook on High for 50 minutes.

2. In a bowl, soak dried cherries in hot water until softened. Once ready, release pressure naturally for 15 minutes. Drain cherries and stir into the tagine. Top with toasted almonds before serving.

Fruity Pork Steaks

Servings: 4
Cooking Time: 30 Minutes
Ingredients:
- 4 pork steaks
- ¼ cup milk
- 8 prunes, pitted
- ½ cup white wine
- 2 apples, peeled, sliced
- ¼ cup heavy cream
- 1 tbsp fruit jelly
- ½ tsp ground ginger
- Salt and pepper to taste

Directions:

1. Place pork, milk, prunes, wine, apples, heavy cream, and ginger in your pressure cooker. Stir and season with salt and pepper. Seal the lid and cook on High Pressure for 15 minutes. Once done, wait 5 minutes and do a quick pressure release. Stir in the jelly and serve.

Desserts & Drinks

After-dinner Boozy Hot Cocoa

Servings: 4
Cooking Time: 5 Minutes
Ingredients:
- 6 cups whole milk
- ¼ cup unsweetened cocoa powder
- ¼ cup mini chocolate chips
- ¼ cup granulated sugar
- ½ cup Irish cream
- ⅛ teaspoon salt
- 2 teaspoons vanilla extract

Directions:
1. Place all ingredients in the Instant Pot. Lock lid.
2. Press the Steam button and adjust time to 5 minutes. When timer beeps, quick-release pressure until float valve drops. Unlock lid. Whisk ingredients to ensure smoothness.
3. Ladle cocoa into four mugs. Serve warm.

Rice Pudding

Servings: 4
Cooking Time: 25 Minutes
Ingredients:
- 1 cup Arborio rice
- 1 ½ cups water
- 1 tablespoon vanilla extract
- 1 cinnamon stick
- 1 tablespoon unsalted butter
- 1 cup golden raisins
- ¼ cup granulated sugar
- ½ cup heavy cream

Directions:
1. Add rice, water, vanilla, cinnamon stick, and butter to the Instant Pot. Lock lid.
2. Press the Manual or Pressure Cook button and adjust time to 20 minutes. When timer beeps, let pressure release naturally for 10 minutes. Quick-release any additional pressure until float valve drops. Press the Cancel button. Unlock lid.
3. Remove cinnamon stick and discard. Stir in raisins, sugar, and heavy cream.
4. Press the Sauté button on the Instant Pot, press Adjust button to change temperature to Less, and simmer unlidded 5 minutes. Serve warm.

Peanut Butter Custards

Servings: 4
Cooking Time: 18 Minutes
Ingredients:
- 4 large egg yolks
- 2 tablespoons granulated sugar
- ⅛ teaspoon salt
- ¼ teaspoon vanilla extract
- 1 ½ cups heavy whipping cream
- ¾ cup peanut butter chips
- 2 cups water

Directions:
1. In a small bowl, whisk together egg yolks, sugar, salt, and vanilla. Set aside.
2. In a small saucepan over medium-low heat, heat cream to a low simmer, about 2 minutes. Whisk a spoonful of warm cream mixture into egg mixture to temper eggs. Then slowly add egg mixture back into saucepan with remaining cream.
3. Add peanut butter chips and continually stir on simmer until chips are melted, about 8–10 minutes. Remove from heat and evenly distribute mixture among four custard ramekins.
4. Add water to the Instant Pot and insert steam rack. Place steamer basket on steam rack. Place ramekins into basket. Lock lid.
5. Press the Manual or Pressure Cook button and adjust time to 6 minutes. When timer beeps, let pressure release naturally for 10 minutes. Quick-release any additional pressure until float valve drops. Unlock lid.
6. Transfer ramekins to a plate and refrigerate covered at least 2 hours or up to overnight. Serve chilled.

Chocolate Quinoa Bowl

Servings: 4
Cooking Time: 15 Minutes
Ingredients:
- 12 squares dark chocolate, shaved
- 2 tbsp cocoa powder
- 1 cup quinoa

- 2 tbsp maple syrup
- ½ tsp vanilla
- A pinch of salt
- 1 tbsp sliced almonds

Directions:

1. Put the quinoa, cocoa powder, maple syrup, vanilla, 2 ¼ cups water, and salt in your Instant Pot. Seal the lid, select Manual, and cook for a minute on High pressure. When ready, allow a natural release for 10 minutes and unlock the lid. Using a fork, fluff the quinoa. Top with almonds and dark chocolate and serve.

Walnut & Pumpkin Tart

Servings: 6
Cooking Time: 70 Minutes
Ingredients:

- 1 cup packed shredded pumpkin
- 3 eggs
- ½ cup sugar
- 1 cup flour
- ½ cup half-and-half
- ¼ cup olive oil
- 1 tsp baking powder
- 1 tsp vanilla extract
- 1 tsp ground cinnamon
- ½ tsp ground nutmeg
- ½ cup chopped walnuts
- 2 cups water
- Frosting:
- 4 oz cream cheese, room temperature
- 8 tbsp butter
- ½ cup confectioners sugar
- ½ tsp vanilla extract
- ½ tsp salt

Directions:

1. In a bowl, beat eggs and sugar to get a smooth mixture. Mix in oil, flour, vanilla extract, cinnamon, half-and-half, baking powder, and nutmeg. Stir well to obtain a fluffy batter. Fold walnuts and pumpkin through the batter. Add batter into a cake pan and cover with aluminum foil. Into the pot, add 1 cup water and set a trivet. Lay cake pan onto the trivet.
2. Seal the lid, select Manual, and cook on High Pressure for 40 minutes. Release pressure naturally for 10 minutes. Beat cream cheese, confectioners' sugar, salt, vanilla, and butter in a bowl until smooth. Place in the refrigerator until needed. Remove cake from the pan and transfer to a wire rack to cool. Over the cake, spread frosting and apply a topping of shredded carrots.

Pie Cups With Fruit Filling

Servings: 6
Cooking Time: 40 Minutes + Chilling Time
Ingredients:

- For the crust:
- 2 cups flour
- ¾ tsp salt
- ¾ cup butter, softened
- 1 tbsp sugar
- ½ cup ice water
- For the filling:
- ½ fresh peach
- ½ cup apples, chopped
- ¼ cup cranberries
- 2 tbsp flour
- 1 tbsp sugar
- ½ tsp cinnamon
- 1 egg yolk, for brushing

Directions:

1. Place flour, salt, butter, sugar, and water in a food processor and pulse until dough becomes crumbly. Remove to a lightly floured work surface. Divide among 4 equal pieces and wrap in plastic foil. Refrigerate for an hour. Place apples, peach, cranberries, flour, sugar, and cinnamon in a bowl. Toss to combine and set aside. Roll each piece into 6-inch round discs. Add 2 tablespoons of the apple mixture at the center of each disc and wrap to form small bowls. Brush each bowl with egg yolk and gently Transfer to an oiled baking dish. Pour 1 cup of water into the pot and insert the trivet. Place the pan on top. Seal the lid, and cook for 25 minutes on High Pressure. Release the pressure naturally. Serve cool.

Banana Bread Pudding

Servings: 4
Cooking Time: 20 Minutes
Ingredients:

- 4 cups cubed French bread, dried out overnight
- 2 small bananas, peeled and sliced
- ¼ cup granulated sugar
- 2 cups whole milk

- 3 large eggs
- ⅛ teaspoon salt
- 3 tablespoons unsalted butter, cut into 4 pats
- 1 ½ cups water

Directions:
1. Grease a 7-cup glass baking dish. Add bread, then banana slices. Sprinkle sugar evenly over bananas. Set aside.
2. In a small bowl, whisk together milk, eggs, and salt. Pour over ingredients in glass baking dish and place butter pats on top.
3. Add water to the Instant Pot and insert steam rack. Place glass baking dish on top of steam rack. Lock lid.
4. Press the Manual or Pressure Cook button and adjust time to 20 minutes. When timer beeps, quick-release pressure until float valve drops. Unlock lid.
5. Remove glass bowl from pot. Transfer to a cooling rack for 30 minutes until set. Serve.

Homemade Lemon Cheesecake

Servings: 6
Cooking Time: 1 Hour + Chilling Time
Ingredients:
- Crust:
- 4 oz graham crackers
- 1 tsp ground cinnamon
- 3 tbsp butter, melted
- Filling:
- 1 lb mascarpone cheese, softened
- ¾ cup sugar
- ¼ cup sour cream, at room temperature
- 2 eggs
- 1 tsp vanilla extract
- 1 tsp lemon zest
- 1 tbsp lemon juice
- A pinch of salt
- 1 cup strawberries, halved

Directions:
1. In a food processor, beat cinnamon and graham crackers to attain a texture almost same as sand; mix in melted butter. Press the crumbs into the bottom of a 7-inch springform pan in an even layer. In a stand mixer, beat sugar, mascarpone cheese, and sour cream for 3 minutes to combine well and have a fluffy and smooth mixture. Scrape the bowl's sides and add eggs, lemon zest, salt, lemon juice, and vanilla. Carry on to beat the mixture until you obtain a consistent color and all ingredients are completely combined. Pour filling over crust.
2. Into the inner pot, add 1 cup water and set in a trivet. Place the springform pan on the trivet. Seal the lid, press Cake, and cook for 40 minutes on High. Release the pressure quickly. Remove the cheesecake and let it cool. Garnish with strawberry halves on top. Use a paring knife to run along the edges between the pan and cheesecake to remove it and set it to a plate. Serve.

Chocolate Glazed Cake

Servings: 6
Cooking Time: 40 Minutes + Chilling Time
Ingredients:
- 3 cups yogurt
- 3 cups flour
- 2 cups granulated sugar
- 1 cup oil
- 2 tsp baking soda
- 3 tbsp cocoa
- For the glaze:
- 7 oz dark chocolate
- 10 tbsp sugar
- 10 tbsp milk
- 5 oz butter, unsalted

Directions:
1. In a bowl, combine yogurt, flour, sugar, oil, baking soda, and cocoa. Beat well with an electric mixer. Transfer a mixture to a large springform pan. Wrap the pan in foil. Insert a trivet in the Instant Pot. Pour in 1 cup water and place the pan on top. Seal the lid and cook for 30 minutes on High Pressure. Do a quick release, remove the pan, and unwrap. Chill well. Microwave the chocolate and whisk in butter, milk, and sugar. Beat well with a mixer and pour the mixture over the cake. Refrigerate for at least two hours before serving.

Catalan-style Crème Brûlée

Servings: 4
Cooking Time: 15 Minutes
Ingredients:
- 5 cups heavy cream
- 8 egg yolks
- 1 cup honey
- 4 tbsp sugar
- 1 vanilla extract

- 1 cup water

Directions:

1. In a bowl, combine heavy cream, egg yolks, vanilla, and honey. Beat well with an electric mixer. Pour the mixture into 4 ramekins. Set aside. Pour water into the pot and insert the trivet. Lower the ramekins on top. Seal the lid and cook for 10 minutes on High Pressure. Do a quick pressure release. Remove the ramekins from the pot and add a tablespoon of sugar to each ramekin. Burn evenly with a culinary torch until brown. Chill well and serve.

Yogurt Cheesecake With Cranberries

Servings: 6
Cooking Time: 45 Minutes + Chilling Time

Ingredients:

- 2 lb Greek yogurt
- 2 cups sugar
- 4 eggs
- 2 tsp lemon zest
- 1 tsp lemon extract
- 1 cheesecake crust
- For topping:
- 7 oz dried cranberries
- 2 tbsp cranberry jam
- 2 tsp lemon zest
- 1 tsp vanilla sugar
- 1 tsp cranberry extract
- ¾ cup lukewarm water

Directions:

1. In a bowl, combine yogurt, sugar, eggs, lemon zest, and lemon extract. With a mixer, beat well until well-combined. Place the crust in a greased cake pan and pour in the filling. Flatten the surface with a spatula. Leave in the fridge for 30 minutes. Combine cranberries, jam, lemon zest, vanilla sugar, cranberry extract, and water in the pot. Simmer for 15 minutes on Sauté. Remove and wipe the pot clean. Fill in 1 cup water and insert a trivet. Set the pan on top of the trivet and pour cranberry topping. Seal the lid and cook for 20 minutes on High Pressure. Do a quick release. Run a sharp knife around the edge of the cheesecake. Refrigerate. Serve and enjoy!

Molten Chocolate Cake

Servings: 6
Cooking Time: 40 Minutes

Ingredients:

- 1 cup butter
- 4 tbsp milk
- 2 tsp vanilla extract
- 1 ½ cups chocolate chips
- 1 ½ cups sugar
- Powdered sugar to garnish
- 7 tbsp flour
- 5 eggs
- 1 cup water

Directions:

1. Grease the cake pan with cooking spray and set aside. Fit the trivet at the pot, and pour in water. In a heatproof bowl, add the butter and chocolate and melt them in the microwave for about 2 minutes. Stir in sugar. Add eggs, milk, and vanilla extract and stir again. Finally, add the flour and stir it until smooth. Pour the batter into the greased cake pan and use a spatula to level it. Place the pan on the trivet, inside the pot, seal the lid, and select Manual at High for 15 minutes.

2. Do a natural pressure release for 10 minutes. Remove the trivet with the pan on it and place the pan on a flat surface. Put a plate over the pan and flip the cake over onto the plate. Pour the powdered sugar in a fine sieve and sift over the cake. Cut the cake into slices and serve.

Steamed Bread Pudding

Servings: 6
Cooking Time: 20 Minutes

Ingredients:

- 4 cups cubed cinnamon-raisin bread, dried out overnight
- 1 apple, peeled, cored, and diced small
- ¼ cup raisins
- 2 cups whole milk
- 3 large eggs
- ½ teaspoon vanilla extract
- 2 tablespoons pure maple syrup
- ¼ teaspoon ground cinnamon
- Pinch of ground nutmeg
- Pinch of sea salt
- 3 tablespoons butter, cut into 3 pats
- 1½ cups water

Directions:

1. Grease a 7-cup glass dish. Add bread, apple, and raisins. Set aside.
2. In a small bowl, whisk together milk, eggs, vanilla, maple syrup, cinnamon, nutmeg, and salt. Pour over bread in glass dish and place pats of butter on top.
3. Pour water into Instant Pot. Set trivet in pot. Place glass dish on top of trivet. Lock lid.
4. Press the Manual button and adjust time to 20 minutes. When timer beeps, quick-release pressure until float valve drops and then unlock lid.
5. Remove glass bowl from the Instant Pot. Transfer to a rack until cooled. Serve.

Best Tiramisu Cheesecake

Servings: 6
Cooking Time: 35 Minutes + Chilling Time
Ingredients:
- 1 ½ cups ladyfingers, crushed
- 1 tbsp Kahlua liquor
- 1 tbsp granulated espresso
- 1 tbsp butter, melted
- 16 oz cream cheese
- 8 oz mascarpone cheese
- 2 tbsp powdered sugar
- ½ cup white sugar
- 1 tbsp cocoa powder
- 1 tsp vanilla extract
- 2 eggs

Directions:
1. In a bowl beat the cream cheese, mascarpone, and white sugar. Gradually beat in the eggs, the powdered sugar, cocoa powder, and vanilla. Combine Kahlua liquor, espresso, butter, and ladyfingers, in another bowl. Press the ladyfinger crust at the bottom. Pour the filling on a greased cake pan. Cover the pan with aluminum foil. Pour 1 cup of water into your pressure cooker and lower a trivet. Place the pan inside and seal the lid. Select Manual and set to 25 minutes at High pressure. Release the pressure quickly. Allow cooling completely.

Strawberry Upside-down Cake

Servings: 4
Cooking Time: 35 Minutes
Ingredients:
- 2 cups diced strawberries
- 1 cup plus 1 tablespoon all-purpose flour, divided
- ⅓ cup plus 1 tablespoon granulated sugar, divided
- 1 large egg
- 2 tablespoons unsalted butter, melted
- 1 teaspoon vanilla extract
- 1 cup ricotta cheese
- 2 teaspoons baking powder
- 1 teaspoon baking soda
- ⅛ teaspoon salt
- 1 ½ cups water

Directions:
1. Grease a 6" cake pan. Place a circle of parchment paper in the bottom.
2. In a medium bowl, toss strawberries in 1 tablespoon flour and 1 tablespoon sugar. Add strawberries to pan in an even layer.
3. In a medium bowl, beat egg. Whisk in butter, ⅓ cup sugar, and vanilla until smooth. Add remaining ingredients, including remaining flour, except water. Pour batter into pan over strawberry layer.
4. Add water to the Instant Pot and insert steam rack. Lower cake pan onto steam rack. Lock lid.
5. Press the Manual or Pressure Cook button and adjust time to 35 minutes. When timer beeps, quick-release pressure until float valve drops. Unlock lid.
6. Remove cake pan from pot and transfer to a cooling rack to cool for 30 minutes. Flip cake onto a serving platter. Remove parchment paper. Slice and serve.

Peanut Butter Chocolate Cheesecake

Servings: 6
Cooking Time: 30 Minutes
Ingredients:
- Crust
- 20 vanilla wafers
- 2 tablespoons creamy peanut butter
- 3 tablespoons melted butter
- Cheesecake Filling
- 12 ounces cream cheese, cubed and room temperature
- 2 tablespoons sour cream, room temperature
- ½ cup sugar
- ¼ cup unsweetened cocoa
- 2 large eggs, room temperature
- 1 teaspoon vanilla extract
- 2 cups water
- ¼ cup mini semisweet chocolate chips

- ¼ cup chopped peanuts
- 2 tablespoons chocolate syrup
- 1 cup whipped cream

Directions:

1. For Crust: Grease a 7" springform pan and set aside.
2. Add vanilla wafers to a food processor and pulse to combine. Add in peanut butter and melted butter. Pulse to blend. Transfer crumb mixture to springform pan and press down along the bottom and about ⅓ of the way up the sides of the pan. Place a square of aluminum foil along the outside bottom of the pan and crimp up around the edges.
3. For Cheesecake Filling: With a hand blender or food processor, cream together cream cheese, sour cream, sugar, and cocoa. Pulse until smooth. Slowly add eggs and vanilla extract. Pulse for another 10 seconds. Scrape the bowl and pulse until batter is smooth. Transfer the batter into springform pan.
4. Pour water into the Instant Pot. Insert the trivet. Set the springform pan on the trivet. Lock lid.
5. Press the Manual button and adjust time to 30 minutes. When timer beeps, quick-release pressure until float valve drops and then unlock lid. Lift pan out of Instant Pot. Garnish immediately with chocolate chips and chopped peanuts. Let cool at room temperature for 10 minutes.
6. The cheesecake will be a little jiggly in the center. Refrigerate for a minimum of 2 hours to allow it to set. Release side pan and serve with drizzled chocolate syrup and whipped cream.

Simple Apple Cinnamon Dessert

Servings: 6
Cooking Time: 30 Minutes
Ingredients:

- Topping:
- ½ cup rolled oats
- ½ cup oat flour
- ½ cup granulated sugar
- ¼ cup olive oil
- Filling:
- 5 apples, cored, and halved
- 2 tbsp arrowroot powder
- ½ cup water
- 1 tsp ground cinnamon
- ¼ tsp ground nutmeg
- ½ tsp vanilla paste

Directions:

1. In a bowl, combine sugar, oat flour, rolled oats, and olive oil to form coarse crumbs. Spoon the apples into the Instant Pot. Mix water with arrowroot powder in a bowl. Stir in nutmeg, cinnamon, and vanilla. Toss in the apples to coat. Apply oat topping to the apples. Seal the lid and cook on High Pressure for 10 minutes. Release the pressure naturally for 10 minutes.

Homemade Walnut Layer Cake

Servings: 6
Cooking Time: 25 Minutes
Ingredients:

- ½ cup vanilla pudding powder
- 3 standard cake crusts
- ¼ cup granulated sugar
- 4 cups milk
- 10.5 oz chocolate chips
- ¼ cup walnuts, minced

Directions:

1. Combine vanilla powder, sugar, and milk in the inner pot. Cook until the pudding thickens, stirring constantly on Sauté. Remove from the steel pot. Place one crust into a springform pan. Pour half of the pudding and sprinkle with minced walnuts and chocolate chips. Cover with another crust and repeat the process. Finish with the final crust and wrap in foil.
2. Insert the trivet, pour in 1 cup of water, and place springform pan on top. Seal the lid and cook for 10 minutes on High Pressure. Do a quick release. Refrigerate.

Grandma's Fruit Compote

Servings: 6
Cooking Time: 45 Minutes
Ingredients:

- 7 oz Turkish figs
- 7 oz fresh cherries
- 7 oz plums
- 3 ½ oz raisins
- 3 large apples, chopped
- 3 tbsp cornstarch
- 1 tsp cinnamon, ground
- 1 cup sugar
- 1 lemon, juiced

Directions:

1. Combine figs, cherries, plums, raisins, apples, cornstarch, cinnamon, sugar, and lemon juice in the Instant Pot. Pour in 3 cups water. Seal the lid and cook for 30 minutes on High pressure. Release the pressure naturally for 10 minutes. Store in big jars.

Easy Lemon Cake

Servings: 6
Cooking Time: 30 Minutes
Ingredients:
- 2 eggs
- 2 cups sugar
- 1 cup vegetable oil
- ½ cup flour
- 1 tsp baking powder
- Lemon topping:
- 1 cup sugar
- 1 cup lemon juice
- 1 tbsp lemon zest
- 1 lemon, sliced

Directions:
1. In a bowl, combine eggs, sugar, oil, and baking powder. Gradually add flour until the mixture is thick and slightly sticky. Shape balls with hands and flatten them to half-inch thick. Place in a baking pan. Pour 1 cup of water, insert a trivet, and lower the pan onto the trivet. Cover the pan with foil and seal the lid. Cook on High Pressure for 20 minutes. Do a quick release. Let cool at room temperature. Add sugar, lemon juice, lemon zest, and lemon slices to the Instant Pot. Press Sauté and stir until the sugar dissolves. Pour the hot topping over the cake.

Simple Lemon Cheesecake

Servings: 6
Cooking Time: 30 Minutes
Ingredients:
- Crust
- 22 vanilla wafer cookies
- 4 tablespoons unsalted butter, melted
- Cheesecake Filling
- 14 ounces cream cheese, cubed and softened
- ½ cup granulated sugar
- ⅛ teaspoon salt
- Juice and zest of 1 large lemon
- 2 large eggs, room temperature
- 1 cup water

Directions:
1. Grease a 7" springform pan and set aside.
2. Add vanilla wafers to a food processor and pulse to combine. Add butter. Pulse to blend. Transfer crumb mixture to prepared springform pan and press down along the bottom and about ⅓ of the way up sides of pan. Place a square of aluminum foil along the outside bottom of pan and crimp up around edges.
3. With a hand blender or food processor, cream together cream cheese, sugar, salt, lemon juice and zest. Pulse until smooth. Slowly add eggs. Pulse another 10 seconds. Scrape bowl and pulse until mixture is smooth.
4. Pour mixture over crust in springform pan.
5. Add water to the Instant Pot and insert steam rack. Set springform pan on steam rack. Lock lid.
6. Press the Manual or Pressure Cook button and adjust time to 30 minutes. When timer beeps, quick-release pressure until float valve drops. Unlock lid.
7. Lift pan out of pot. Let cool at room temperature 10 minutes. The cheesecake will be a little jiggly in the center. Refrigerate a minimum of 2 hours or up to overnight to allow it to set. Release sides of pan and serve.

Quick Coconut Treat With Pears

Servings: 2
Cooking Time: 15 Minutes
Ingredients:
- ¼ cup flour
- 1 cup coconut milk
- 2 pears, peeled and diced
- ¼ cup shredded coconut

Directions:
1. Combine flour, milk, pears, and shredded coconut in your Pressure cooker. Seal the lid, select Pressure Cook and set the timer to 5 minutes at High pressure. When ready, do a quick pressure release. Divide the mixture between two bowls. Serve.

Root Beer Float Cupcakes

Servings: 12
Cooking Time: 18 Minutes
Ingredients:
- Cupcakes
- ½ box moist vanilla cake mix
- 6 ounces (½ can) root beer
- 2 cups water
- Vanilla Buttercream

- 1 cup confectioners' sugar
- ⅓ cup unsalted butter, softened
- ½ teaspoon vanilla extract
- 1 tablespoon whole milk

Directions:
1. Grease twelve silicone cupcake liners.
2. In a medium bowl, combine cake mix and root beer. Spoon mixture into cupcake liners.
3. Add water to the Instant Pot and insert steam rack. Place six cupcake liners on steam rack. Lock lid.
4. Press the Manual or Pressure Cook button and adjust time to 9 minutes. When timer beeps, quick-release pressure until float valve drops. Unlock lid. Transfer cupcakes to a cooling rack. Repeat cooking process with remaining six cupcake liners.
5. To make buttercream, cream together vanilla buttercream ingredients in a medium mixing bowl. If buttercream is too loose, add a little more confectioners' sugar. If buttercream is too thick, add a little more milk.
6. Let cupcakes cool for at least 30 minutes until they reach room temperature, then spread buttercream on cooled cupcakes. Serve.

Simple Apple Cider With Orange Juice

Servings: 6
Cooking Time: 20 Minutes
Ingredients:
- 6 green apples, chopped
- ¼ cup orange juice
- 2 cinnamon sticks

Directions:
1. In a blender, add orange juice, apples, and 3 cups water and blend until smooth; use a fine-mesh strainer to strain and press using a spoon. Get rid of the pulp. In the pot, mix the apple puree and cinnamon sticks. Seal the lid and cook for 10 minutes on High Pressure. Release the Pressure naturally. Strain again and do away with the solids.

Pineapple Upside-down Cake

Servings: 4
Cooking Time: 35 Minutes
Ingredients:
- ½ cup drained crushed pineapple
- 12 maraschino cherries
- 1 large egg
- 2 tablespoons melted butter
- ⅓ cup sugar
- 1 teaspoon vanilla extract
- 1 cup ricotta cheese
- 1 cup flour
- 2 teaspoons baking powder
- 1 teaspoon baking soda
- Pinch of salt
- 1½ cups water

Directions:
1. Grease a 6" cake pan. Place a circle of parchment paper in the bottom. Add a layer of pineapple and distribute cherries evenly among the pineapple.
2. In a medium bowl, beat egg. Whisk in butter, sugar, and vanilla until smooth. Add remaining ingredients except water. Pour into pan over pineapple and cherries.
3. Pour water into Instant Pot. Add trivet. Lower cake pan onto trivet. Lock lid.
4. Press the Manual button and adjust time to 35 minutes. When the timer beeps, quick-release pressure until float valve drops and then unlock lid.
5. Remove cake pan from the pot and transfer to a rack to cool. Flip cake onto a serving platter. Remove parchment paper. Slice and serve.

Stuffed Apples

Servings: 4
Cooking Time: 10 Minutes
Ingredients:
- 4 Granny Smith apples
- 5 tablespoons unsalted butter, softened
- 2 teaspoons ground cinnamon
- ¼ cup packed light brown sugar
- ¼ teaspoon vanilla extract
- ¼ cup chopped walnuts
- ⅛ teaspoon salt
- 2 cups water

Directions:
1. Core apples, leaving some skin on bottom of hole to hold filling in place. Using a paring knife, remove just a little more of the apple center for a bigger area to fill.
2. In a medium bowl, combine butter, cinnamon, brown sugar, vanilla, walnuts, and salt. Stuff apples with this mixture. Place apples in a 7-cup baking dish.

3. Add water to the Instant Pot and insert steam rack. Place baking dish on steam rack.
4. Press the Manual or Pressure Cook button and adjust time to 10 minutes. When timer beeps, quick-release pressure until float valve drops. Unlock lid.
5. Allow apples to cool in pot 20 minutes. Serve warm.

Pumpkin Cheesecake

Servings: 6
Cooking Time: 30 Minutes
Ingredients:
- Crust
- 20 gingersnaps
- 3 tablespoons melted butter
- Cheesecake Filling
- 1 cup pumpkin purée
- 8 ounces cream cheese, cubed and room temperature
- 2 tablespoons sour cream, room temperature
- ½ cup sugar
- Pinch of salt
- 2 large eggs, room temperature
- ¼ teaspoon ground cinnamon
- ⅛ teaspoon ground nutmeg
- ½ teaspoon vanilla extract
- 2 cups water

Directions:
1. Grease a 7" springform pan and set aside.
2. For Crust: Add gingersnaps to a food processor and pulse to combine. Add in melted butter and pulse to blend. Transfer crumb mixture to springform pan and press down along the bottom and about ⅓ of the way up the sides of the pan. Place a square of aluminum foil along the outside bottom of the pan and crimp up around the edges.
3. For Cheesecake Filling: With a hand blender or food processor, cream together pumpkin, cream cheese, sour cream, sugar, and salt. Pulse until smooth. Slowly add eggs, cinnamon, nutmeg, and vanilla. Pulse for another 10 seconds. Scrape the bowl and pulse until batter is smooth.
4. Transfer the batter into springform pan.
5. Pour water into the Instant Pot. Insert the trivet. Set the springform pan on the trivet. Lock lid.
6. Press the Manual button and adjust time to 30 minutes. When timer beeps, quick-release pressure until float valve drops and then unlock lid. Lift pan out of Instant Pot. Let cool at room temperature for 10 minutes.
7. The cheesecake will be a little jiggly in the center. Refrigerate for a minimum of 2 hours to allow it to set. Release side pan and serve.

Lemon-apricot Compote

Servings: 6
Cooking Time: 20 Minutes
Ingredients:
- 2 lb fresh apricots, sliced
- 1 lb sugar
- 2 tbsp lemon zest
- 1 tsp ground nutmeg
- 10 cups water

Directions:
1. Add apricots, sugar, water, nutmeg, and lemon zest. Cook, stirring occasionally until half of the water evaporates, on Sauté. Press Cancel and transfer the apricots and the remaining liquid into glass jars. Let cool. Refrigerate.

Plum & Almond Dessert

Servings: 6
Cooking Time: 1 Hour 50 Minutes
Ingredients:
- 6 lb sweet ripe plums, pits removed and halved
- 2 cups white sugar
- 1 cup almond flakes

Directions:
1. Drizzle the plums with sugar. Toss to coat. Let it stand for about 1 hour to allow plums to soak up the sugar. Transfer the plum mixture to the Instant Pot and pour 1 cup of water. Seal the lid and cook on High Pressure for 30 minutes. Allow the Pressure to release naturally for 10 minutes. Serve topped with almond flakes.

Creme Caramel With Whipped Cream

Servings: 4
Cooking Time: 30 Minutes + Cooling Time
Ingredients:
- ½ cup granulated sugar
- 4 tbsp caramel syrup
- 3 eggs
- ½ tsp vanilla extract
- ½ tbsp milk
- 5 oz whipping cream

Directions:

1. Combine milk, whipping cream, and vanilla extract in your Instant Pot. Press Sauté, and cook for 5 minutes, or until small bubbles form. Set aside. Using an electric mixer, whisk the eggs and sugar. Gradually add the cream mixture and whisk until well combined. Divide the caramel syrup between 4 ramekins. Fill with egg mixture and place them on the trivet. Pour in 1 cup water. Seal the lid and cook for 15 minutes on High Pressure. Do a quick release. Remove the ramekins and cool.

Homemade Spanish-style Horchata

Servings: 4
Cooking Time: 20 Minutes
Ingredients:

- 4 cups cold water
- ½ cup short-grain rice
- ¼ stick cinnamon
- Zest from 1 lemon
- 2 tbsp sugar
- 1 tbsp cinnamon powder

Directions:

1. In the pot, combine cinnamon stick, rice and 2 cups of water. Seal the lid cook on High Pressure for 5 minutes. Release pressure naturally for 10 minutes. In a blender, puree the rice mixture with the lemon zest and sugar. Strain the blended mixture into the remaining water. Mix well and place in the refrigerator until ready for serving. Serve sprinkled with cinnamon.

APPENDIX A: Measurement

BASIC KITCHEN CONVERSIONS & EQUIVALENTS DRY MEASUREMENTS CONVERSION CHART

3 TEASPOONS = 1 TABLESPOON = 1/16 CUP

6 TEASPOONS = 2 TABLESPOONS = 1/8 CUP

12 TEASPOONS = 4 TABLESPOONS = 1/4 CUP

24 TEASPOONS = 8 TABLESPOONS = 1/2 CUP

36 TEASPOONS = 12 TABLESPOONS = 3/4 CUP

48 TEASPOONS = 16 TABLESPOONS = 1 CUP

METRIC TO US COOKING CONVERSIONS OVEN TEMPERATURES

120 ° C = 250 ° F 160 ° C = 320 ° F 180° C = 350 ° F 205 ° C = 400 ° F 220 ° C = 425 ° F

LIQUID MEASUREMENTS CONVERSION CHART

8 FLUID OUNCES = 1 CUP = 1/2 PINT = 1/4 QUART

16 FLUID OUNCES = 2 CUPS = 1 PINT = 1/2 QUART

32 FLUID OUNCES = 4 CUPS = 2 PINTS = 1 QUART = 1/4 GALLON

128 FLUID OUNCES = 16 CUPS = 8 PINTS = 4 QUARTS = 1 GALLON

BAKING IN GRAMS

1 CUP FLOUR = 140 GRAMS

1 CUP SUGAR = 150 GRAMS

1 CUP POWDERED SUGAR = 160 GRAMS

1 CUP HEAVY CREAM = 235 GRAMS

VOLUME

1 MILLILITER = 1/5 TEASPOON

5 ML = 1 TEASPOON

15 ML = 1 TABLESPOON

240 ML = 1 CUP OR 8 FLUID OUNCES

1 LITER = 34 FL. OUNCES

WEIGHT

1 GRAM = .035 OUNCES

100 GRAMS = 3.5 OUNCES

500 GRAMS = 1.1 POUNDS

1 KILOGRAM = 35 OUNCES

US TO METRIC COOKING CONVERSIONS

1/5 TSP = 1 ML

1 TSP = 5 ML

1 TBSP = 15 ML

1 FL OUNCE = 30 ML

1 CUP = 237 ML

1 PINT (2 CUPS) = 473 ML

1 QUART (4 CUPS) = .95 LITER

1 GALLON (16 CUPS) = 3.8 LITERS

1 OZ = 28 GRAMS

1 POUND = 454 GRAMS

BUTTER

1 CUP BUTTER = 2 STICKS = 8 OUNCES = 230 GRAMS = 8 TABLESPOONS

WHAT DOES 1 CUP EQUAL

1 CUP = 8 FLUID OUNCES

1 CUP = 16 TABLESPOONS

1 CUP = 48 TEASPOONS

1 CUP = 1/2 PINT

1 CUP = 1/4 QUART

1 CUP = 1/16 GALLON

1 CUP = 240 ML

BAKING PAN CONVERSIONS

1 CUP ALL-PURPOSE FLOUR = 4.5 OZ

1 CUP ROLLED OATS = 3 OZ 1 LARGE EGG = 1.7 OZ

1 CUP BUTTER = 8 OZ 1 CUP MILK = 8 OZ

1 CUP HEAVY CREAM = 8.4 OZ

1 CUP GRANULATED SUGAR = 7.1 OZ

1 CUP PACKED BROWN SUGAR = 7.75 OZ

1 CUP VEGETABLE OIL = 7.7 OZ

1 CUP UNSIFTED POWDERED SUGAR = 4.4 OZ

BAKING PAN CONVERSIONS

9-INCH ROUND CAKE PAN = 12 CUPS

10-INCH TUBE PAN = 16 CUPS

11-INCH BUNDT PAN = 12 CUPS

9-INCH SPRINGFORM PAN = 10 CUPS

9 X 5 INCH LOAF PAN = 8 CUPS

9-INCH SQUARE PAN = 8 CUPS

APPENDIX B: Recipes Index

A

Acorn Squash With Sweet Glaze 41
After-dinner Boozy Hot Cocoa 79
Apricot Jam-glazed Ham 76
Asian-style Chicken Soup 28
Asparagus Pasta With Pesto Sauce 37

B

Bacon Cheddar Scrambled Egg Muffins 21
Bacon Onion Cheddar Frittata 14
Banana & Vanilla Pancakes 15
Banana Bread Pudding 80
Banana Nut Bread Oatmeal 16
Basic Basmati White Rice 36
Basil Clams With Garlic & White Wine 51
Beanless Chili 30
Beef Arancini With Potatoes 70
Beef Pasta Alla Parmigiana 33
Beef Shawarma Bowls 77
Best Italian Chicken Balls 65
Best Tiramisu Cheesecake 83
Black Bean Slider Patties 41
Blueberry-oat Muffins 18
Boston Baked Beans 34
Breakfast Frittata 21
Broccoli & Pancetta Carbonara 37
Bulgur Pilaf With Roasted Bell Peppers 38
Buttermilk Cornish Game Hens 67
Buttery Cod With Scallions 51

C

Cajun Pork Carnitas 75
Cajun Red Beans 39
California Frittata Bake 20
Cannellini Beans With Garlic & Leeks 43
Carnitas Lettuce Wraps 70
Carrot & Chickpea Boil With Tomatoes 49
Carrot Casserole With Beef & Potato 70
Catalan-style Crème Brûlée 81

Cauliflower & Potato Curry With Cilantro 44
Cauliflower & Potato Soup With Parsley 23
Cauliflower Charcuterie 48
Cauliflower Rice With Peas & Chili 41
Celery & Red Bean Stew 47
Cheddar Cheese Sauce With Broccoli 46
Cheeseburger Macaroni 33
Cheesy Shrimp Scampi 55
Chicken & Broccoli Rice 34
Chicken & Noodle Soup 30
Chicken & Quinoa Soup 64
Chicken & Vegetable Stew 66
Chicken Alla Diavola 66
Chicken Drumsticks In Sriracha Sauce 65
Chicken Fricassee 63
Chicken Salad 62
Chicken Sandwiches With Barbecue Sauce 18
Chicken Taco Salad Bowls 59
Chicken Wings In Yogurt-garlic Sauce 59
Chicken With Honey-lime Sauce 66
Chickpea & Jalapeño Chicken 38
Chili Corn On The Cob 26
Chili Squid 57
Chinese Shrimp With Green Beans 51
Chocolate Glazed Cake 81
Chocolate Quinoa Bowl 79
Chorizo Soup With Roasted Tomatoes 23
Chorizo With Macaroni & Cheddar Cheese 73
Cilantro Cod On Millet With Peppers 52
Cinnamon Roll Doughnut Holes 15
Classic Pork Goulash 76
Coconut Milk Yogurt With Honey 47
Cranberry Millet Pilaf 33
Creamed Crab 57
Creamed Lentils 38
Creamy Creamed Corn 25
Creamy Mascarpone Chicken 67
Creme Caramel With Whipped Cream 87
Creole Seafood Gumbo 56
Crispy Bacon & Bean Chicken 62
Crushed Potatoes With Aioli 23
Crustless Crab Quiche 17
Crustless Power Quiche 22
Cumin Chicken With Capers 62
Cumin Pork Chops With Peach Sauce 75

D

Delicious Mushroom Goulash 46
Delicious Pork & Garbanzo Bean Chili 23
Dijon Mustard Chicken Breast 60

E

Easy Lemon Cake 85
Easy Pesto Chicken And Red Potatoes 65
Easy Seafood Paella 50
Easy Tahini Sweet Potato Mash 42
Egg Muffins To Go 16
Eggplant & Beef Stew With Parmesan 77
English Vegetable Potage 44

F

Fennel Chicken With Tomato Sauce 61
Four Cheeses Party Pizza 29
Frittata With Vegetables & Cheese 24
Fruity Pork Steaks 78

G

Galician-style Octopus 51
Garlic & Thyme Pork 75
Garlic Mushroom Polenta 35
Garlicky Mashed Root Vegetables 25
Goat Cheese & Beef Steak Salad 27
Grandma's Asparagus With Feta & Lemon 42
Grandma's Fruit Compote 84
Greek Yogurt With Honey & Walnuts 21
Green Pea & Beef Ragout 69

H

Ham And Swiss Muffin Frittatas 20
Happy Dip 26
Hard-"boiled" Eggs 17
Hawaiian Rice 32
Herbed Poached Salmon 53
Herby Chicken With Peach Gravy 64
Herby Crab Legs With Lemon 50
Herby Trout With Farro & Green Beans 54
Homemade Gazpacho Soup 48
Homemade Lemon Cheesecake 81
Homemade Spanish-style Horchata 88

Homemade Vichyssoise Soup With Chives 27
Homemade Walnut Layer Cake 84
Honey Butternut Squash Cake Oatmeal 18
Honey Coconut Rice 39
Honey-lemon Chicken With Vegetables 59
Hot Tofu Meatballs 43
Hungarian-style Turkey Stew 59

I

Indian-style Chicken 64
Insalata Caprese Chicken Bowls 67
Italian Meatballs With Pomodoro Sauce 71
Italian-style Brussels Sprouts 27

J

Jalapeño Shrimp With Herbs & Lemon 55

K

Kiwi Steel Cut Oatmeal 37
Korean Short Ribs 71

L

Lemon-apricot Compote 87
Lemony Pancake Bites With Blueberry Syrup 14
Lime Brown Rice 40
Littleneck Clams In Garlic Wine Broth 53
Low-country Boil 54

M

Mediterranean Cod With Capers 50
Mediterranean Soup With Tortellini 29
Molten Chocolate Cake 82
Mom's Black-eyed Peas With Garlic & Kale 36
Mongolian Beef Bbq 72
Moroccan Beef & Cherry Stew 77
Mushroom & Ricotta Cheese Manicotti 48
Mussels With Lemon & White Wine 56
Mustard Macaroni & Cheese 36

N

Nutty Potatoes 28

O

One-pot Mexican Rice 32
Orange Roughy With Zucchini 56

P

Paprika Salmon With Dill Sauce 50
Parmesan Risotto 36
Parmesan Topped Vegetable Mash 48
Parsley Lentil Soup With Vegetables 45
Party Shrimp With & Rice Veggies 52
Pea & Beef Stew 28
Peachy Cream Oats 22
Peanut Butter Chocolate Cheesecake 83
Peanut Butter Custards 79
Picante Chicken Wings 28
Pie Cups With Fruit Filling 80
Pineapple Upside-down Cake 86
Plum & Almond Dessert 87
Pork Ribs With Onions 26
Potato & Broccoli Soup With Rosemary 30
Primavera Egg Noodles 32
Provençal Rice 35
Pulled Bbq Beef 74
Pumpkin & Wild Rice Cajun Chicken 61
Pumpkin Cheesecake 87
Pumpkin Spice Latte French Toast Casserole 19
Pumpkin Steel Cut Oats With Cinnamon 16

Q

Quick Cassoulet 46
Quick Coconut Treat With Pears 85
Quick French-style Lamb With Sesame 74
Quick Shrimp Gumbo With Sausage 55
Quinoa Bowls With Broccoli & Pesto 33
Quinoa With Brussels Sprouts & Broccoli 46

R

Red Onion Trout Fillets With Olives 56
Red Wine Beef & Vegetable Hotpot 76
Red Wine Squid 58
Rice & Chicken Soup 35
Rice & Red Bean Pot 35
Rice Pudding 79
Risotto With Spring Vegetables & Shrimp 32

Roman Stewed Beans With Tomatoes 45
Root Beer Float Cupcakes 85
Rosemary Chicken With Asparagus Sauce 61

S

Sambal Beef Noodles 73
Sausage & Egg Casserole 31
Sausage And Sweet Potato Hash 15
Savory Butternut Squash Soup 24
Savory Cod Fillets In Maple-lemon Sauce 54
Savory Orange Chicken 62
Savory Roast Beef Sandwiches 16
Savory Spinach With Mashed Potatoes 45
Seafood Pilaf 55
Seasoned Black Beans 47
Seasoned Boneless Pork Loin 70
Shroomy Meatballs 69
Simple Apple Cider With Orange Juice 86
Simple Apple Cinnamon Dessert 84
Simple Lemon Cheesecake 85
South American Pot 39
Southern Pot Roast With Pepperoncini 76
Sparerib Nachos 29
Speedy Soft-boiled Eggs 21
Spiced Pork With Orange & Cinnamon 69
Spicy Chicken Chili 27
Spicy Ground Turkey Chili With Vegetables 63
Spicy Lamb & Bean Chili 72
Spicy Linguine With Cherry Tomato & Basil 34
Spicy Shiitake Mushrooms With Potatoes 43
Spicy Split Pea Stew 42
Steamed Bread Pudding 82
Steamed Broccoli 29
Steamed Halibut Packets 52
Steamed Shrimp And Asparagus 53
Strawberry Jam 19
Strawberry Upside-down Cake 83
Stuffed Apples 86
Stuffed Bell Peppers 43
Stuffed Tench With Herbs & Lemon 53
Sumac Red Potatoes 26
Sweet & Spicy Bbq Chicken 65
Sweet Potato Chili 45
Sweet Potato Morning Hash 19

T

Tandoori Pork Butt 74
Tangy Egg Snacks 24
Tasty Chicken Breasts With Bbq Sauce 68
Tasty Indian Chicken Curry 63
T-bone Steaks With Basil & Mustard 72
Tex-mex Breakfast 17
Tex-mex Quinoa 44
Tilapia Fillets With Hazelnut Crust 52
Tofu Hash Brown Breakfast 15
Tomato Mozzarella Basil Egg Bites 20
Traditional Italian Pesto 42
Trail Mix Oatmeal 22
Trout In Herb Sauce 57
Turkey Cakes With Ginger Gravy 60
Turkey Sausage With Brussels Sprouts 60
Twice-baked Potatoes 25

V

Vanilla Chai Latte Oatmeal 19
Vegan Sloppy Joe's 41
Vegetable & Lamb Casserole 72
Vegetable Casserole With Smoked Bacon 71
Vegetarian Soup With White Beans 26
Vietnamese-style Rice Noodle Soup 73

W

Walnut & Pumpkin Tart 80
Weeknight Baked Beans 39
Western Omelet Casserole 14

Y

Yogurt Cheesecake With Cranberries 82

Z

Ziti Green Minestrone 37